Just Three Words

Poems by
Kevin Randall

M&B Global Solutions Inc.

Just Three Words

Copyright © 2016 Kevin Randall

First Edition
All rights reserved. With the exception of quoting brief passages for the purposes of review, no part of this publication may be reproduced without prior written permission from the Publisher or copyright holder. The information in this book is true and complete to the best of our knowledge.

Disclaimer
The views expressed in this work are solely those of the author and copyright holder and do not necessarily reflect the views of the publisher, and the publisher hereby disclaims any responsibility for them. In the event you use any of the information in this book for yourself, which is your constitutional right, the author, the copyright holder and the publisher assume no responsibility for your actions.

ISBN 10: 1-942731-21-3
ISBN 13: 978-1-942-731-21-4

Published by M&B Global Solutions Inc.
Green Bay, Wisconsin (USA)

Dedication

In loving memory to Mom, Georgia, and Papa Joe, who taught me faith, love, and life lessons by what they did and didn't do. Loving thanks also to other family and friends!

Be Safe. Be Good. Be Kool.

Just Three Words: "I Love You!"

Contents

Acknowledgements ix
Poet's Preface Prose x
What I'm Thinking xii

Part I: Enlighten the Mind (Secret Senses Shine) 1
Treasures of Autumn 2
Candy Sunshine Sparkles 4
My Little Knight 6
Eyes of Red 8
Secrets of Joy 10
Miss the Call 12
I Was You 14
Wave of Hands 16
Rush of Time 19
Halloween Haunting Horror 22
Knock on Wood 26
Magic Wand Spell 28
Don Those Shoes 30
"Closer" Versus "Loser" 35
There Once Was 36
Some Midpoint View 38
Respect Her Privacy 40
Three Times Soliloquy 42
My Backyard Swing 44
Give Me Three 48
Big Girl Hat! 50
Gang's All Here 52
Trite Cliches Tripe 56
... one small blurb 60
What Neighbors Say 62
Old Brings New 64
Cross-Stich Prose Potpourri 66

Part II: Inspire the Heart (Live Love Laugh) 69
Springtime Left Behind 70
This Empty Chair 72
Just Gotta Be! 75
... don't call me 76
Plane + Pilot = Insane?! 79
Mondays Do Happen 81
Mailbox Mayhem Madness 83
Every Body Lookin' 86
Against the Grain 88
My Friend Jack 90
Best Kept Secret 92
Two Tables Over 96
Gravel Hill Cabin 100
Share a Moment 102
Perils of Paradox 104
Bus Bingo Boogie 106
Just In Time 109
In Your Circle 110
She's So Amazing 112
I'm So Free 113
Accept Loves Memory 114

Continued

Part III: Enrich the Soul (Faith Fortitude Forever) ..117
Fire Flare Flame 118
His True Magic 121
Gift of Change 123
All is Silent 127
Grand! Grand! Grand! 128
Lost Family Prayer 131
With Angel's Care 132
Yes! No. Maybe? 134
Peace Quest March 136
Seasons of Beauty 138
Live-On Legacy 140
Mind - Heart - Soul 142
My Prayer Friend 144
My Daily Devotions 146
Kids Teach Us 150

The Free Spirits (Epigram) 153

About the Author 165

Acknowledgements

A gigantic THANK YOU to my publishers, Bonnie Groessl and Mike Dauplaise at M&B Global Solutions Inc., who mentored me through my first literary project!

Special thanks to Darlene Bock, a fellow Western Illinois University alum, on her professional illustrations that added just the right touch to some of these poetry pieces. Please check out her phenomenal portfolio and award-winning, laudable art repertoire on her website: http://www.darlenebock.com/.

Hats off and a shout out to my other unique illustration contributors for "Don Those Shoes": grandchildren Jacob Morrissette and William Eland, and to talented, joyful bus riders: Kosa Kaquatosh, Mandy Kaquatosh, Laina Pamanet, Emily Piepkorn, Molly Piepkorn, Makyah Skenadore, Laney Van Straten, and Madelyn Van Straten. You rock!

I also would like to acknowledge:

Brownlow Publishing Company, for its 1993 daily calender *Heart To Heart* and use of its enriching quotes.

Father Tim, for your special approval epigram blessing! Also, definitely for your awe-inspiring, faith-provocative, spiritually uplifting messages of spreading The Word! Definite Divine Discipleship!

NIV Men's Devotional Bible, 1993 international version, for The Good Word.

*Our Daily Bread ... Personal & Family Devotion*s, for those very inspiring daily devotions!

Heartfelt gratitude to my special Earth Angels of good hope (new hope!), who have shared love, laughs and life! You know who you are.

Keep The Faith
Pass It On
Keep Smilin'!

Kevin Randall

Poet's Preface Prose

When I began writing in my early-grade youth, I took my clues from my surroundings. I didn't have many playmates and learned to stay keenly focused on who, what and where – the continual questions found in my guarded "aura" force field.

I grew up on a Midwestern farm with a strong family unit. The country school was our biggest common ally, and we shared a faith-filled dedication to the Catholic Church.

As I think back, one advantage I had in honing my literary skills was I got to explore the world thru reading. Mom, being a school librarian, brought home a few books, but the greatest gift was when she brought home the grand prize, the *Weekly Reader* magazine! Mom didn't let on, but I think she got a big kick out of watching me do word puzzles and tackle the crossword puzzle. To this day, that is a family tradition that is carried on. Heck, Dad, "Papa Joe," continued with hunting out word searches into his 90s.

I still do puzzles daily, intermixed with scrambled words and Sodoku, being that I am a numbers guy, too. I write all in pen now. Shhh! Heaven forbid, dear Mom, rest her soul, would cringe at my pen print, because her cardinal rules were to always use pencil and always print cap letters, and stay away from contractions, slang, capital words, etc. But look how the word puzzle world has evolved. Today's puzzle creators break down the doors on all those rules and more with the use of foreign languages, Greek letters and abbreviations.

Growing up with lots of trivia available in my formative years helped me form some spelling and writing skills. When I am purely stumped, I do ask family and friends to lend me some letters to complete the puzzle at hand. I challenge myself on how fast I can complete each puzzle. And, I can be trusted not to cheat too oft. It's those darn literary quotes for puzzle clues that drive me crazy! Makes you want to scream, "Help me!"

Speaking of that, the goal of this book is to be informative while in projecting "a moral to the story." It was suggested I include a few surprises for the audience. (My personal aside here: how crazy is it that non-rhyming prose is considered poetry, too?) I am a purist. It has to rhyme, with a beat of time, to be a poem, like a limerick. I duly respect those who can pull off all types, especially those who have a more sophisticated mind, body, soul in their writings. They give the audience what they want. My audience is you, too, with one small caveat: it's really mainly me! Not being egotist, it's just another form of getting the message told.

I write with a certain musical beat in my head. I ask others for the inspiration of tag lines by giving me "just three words," each unrelated in subject matter. Since I also ask them to tell me something about themselves, I can boast of composing a personalized product. The best part is I proudly read it to them in unfinished form. My initial efforts can be wordy and complicated, with imperfect speech breaks, punctuation, and proper tenses, etc.

Now you know what I was thinking as I compiled this book, garnering up all my little quotes found on Post-it notes, in school-style, lined notebook paper. I am still uncovering scratch paper writings and even old newspaper clippings from years/ decades ago (on the narrow margins of, what else, crossword cutouts!) and on other paper scraps from unrelated subjects.

My desire is for you to read my prose carefully at least twice. Each poem includes a brief introduction on what I was mentally focused on when I prepared each work. Even though many themed subjects may seem duplicated, my intent is to give a varying, purposeful moral to each story. Hopefully, you enjoy reading "Just Three Words," just as much as I enjoyed writing such prose for you and me. Read On, Friend!

What I'm Thinking

To lend you a clue, or two, or three, for an easier read of each literary piece, I am including a forerunner passage on "What I'm Thinking" – where my mindset was at to prepare for each particular prose composition.

Please, take the time to peruse each poem three times to let it sink in for your mind, heart, soul to be touched. My goal is to have a "moral of the story" message to result from each piece of prose.

Hopefully you will get the point, then either, Use It, Lose It, or even Pass It on to a friend.

Now, since we all have a story to tell, it's your turn to tell me "What You're Thinking."

Part I

Enlighten The Mind

(Secret Senses Shine)

Kevin Randall

"Treasures of Autumn"

1) We sometimes take all of Mother Nature's beauty for granted; we should be more aware of our surroundings; 2) I lost a finger in an accident years ago, and for some time, I got 'phantom' feelings in its place. In a parallel manner, I feel when one of my senses is 'lost' or diminished, then my other senses seemingly become enhanced to compensate; 3) NOW, is the time to take in all of Nature's senses and truly enjoy them more!

"Look deep into Nature, and then you will understand everything better." ~ Albert Einstein

Under the bridge, over the fall
Water runs so deep, like memories to recall.
Shivering silver against a backdrop of blue,
Quivering river ripple adds a crop of misty hue.

The skyline blends in where an opening does appear
But, then trends of pitch black shadows bring on quiet fear.
Seeing the sun, near to a close, as wandering park visitors stroll through
Feeding animals here from the benches is where dark inquisitors are
    found, too.

"Shush, quiet now!" Why, I see the dancing stars move toward the bank!
Hushed mother of ducklings signals warnings in formation, while swans
    are at their flank.
Could there yet be such a serene sight of pure beauty?
Trees lined in colored ragin' light, waving ev'er so gently!

The sounds of transits rumble in the distance.
Stirs me back to reality with mumbled resistance.
Let me absorb again the odors lifting from a nearby smoky fire
Filling all my senses on this autumn day, rejuvenating my life's desire.

Even tho' the temp drops and the park does empty,
Amidst all these "props of senses" that sure fills my soul aplenty.
Amazingly, nice delight is found in Nature's sampled pleasures.
Ultimately, we get to share them, arisen through God's simple autumn
    treasures!

Kevin Randall

"Candy Sunshine Sparkles"

1) Many folks have favorite memories of visiting Grandma's house; 2) Mine? Just happened to be focused on those rare times, like when Grandma would let us kids play in the 'locked off' fancy sitting room, reserved for adult company; 3) Then, to really make our visit so special, she would allow us all to pick out a sparkling wrapped candy dish treat to "make our day!" Mmmmmm!!

"Candy Sunshine Sparkles"

There's a tale to be told.
How sparkled sweets unfold.
    Reach in the dish,
    Take each piece out as a wish,
    And suckle them, no doubt, so bold.

Sunshine sparkles, warms the cold.
    Gives us all hope and tastes to behold.
Sunrays shine down upon,
    As clouds cover up and do hang on.
Still, sweets sparkle from the dish mold.

Candy never seems to grow old.
    How each nugget twinkles when sold.
    Melts, as it tingles, like pure gold.
    Over the tongue, through the gum;
    Lookout stomach, here it comes.
    Gems of candy sunshine sparkles now told!

Kevin Randall

"My Little Knight"

1) Growing up, I had of a few nightmare dreams; 2) To keep the scary times away, I had a small flashlight next to my bed; 3) That brave little light never failed to help me sleep safe, secure, and snuggled tight!

"My Little Knight"

There's a little flashlight, standing guard by my sleeping bed.
I am content, when it's in sight, being not far from my head.
Amazing, how it wields such a beam so bright, when the power "ON" is fed.
A blazing, it shields me from scary fright, the spooky sounds that I dread.

He shines his light when I hear a hooting owl, or a howling bark.
He's so divine to be near each night, with his sprawling sentry spark.
How, I feel secure with my little flashlight; wrestling with pillow goblins when I sleep.
Now, my nightmares fade to my delight; nestling in, so that ghosts never take their leap.

I am very thankful for such a brave lighting gift.
He's ever watchful, always being on a guarding shift.
Dozing, with my little flashlight, My Little Knight, although well-tested, rarely goes adrift.
Awaking in the morning light, I slept tight, well-rested through his safety light lift.

He's fending off any bad dream fright, each and every eerie night.
I am e'er depending upon My Little Knight, who forever beams through my little flashlight!

"Eyes of Red"

1) Numerous life situations can lead to red eyes; 2) No matter the definition, it can be quite a prevalent term. So try to avoid those trying times of getting red eyes; 3) Red eyes may have a negative connotation; however, maybe the 'best red eye' is the one you catch getting home?

"A happy heart can make the face cheerful, but a heavy heart can break the spirit." ~ Proverbs 15:13

You look so tired, your eyes so red.
Staying up so wired, taking any med?
Crazy fight you had . . . maybe they bled.
Crying, might you be mad on something said?

Eyes of red . . .
Ouch, like aiming a needle pulling thread.
Oh! That wicked mid-storm, awaiting what is 'bout to dread.
Blushing at errs recanted, changes replayed on "what if . . ." instead.
Rushing passengers to flights; and, how they sped!

Eyes of red . . .
Ill enough seen, can't get out of bed.
Silver screen makes us fuzzy as we tread.
Shyness, exhumes us to be so timid;
Yet, staying focused on the prize so vivid.

Just Three Words

Eyes of red . . .
Bull's-eyes aimed at, and, dragons sleighed, (that's what we read.)
Pondering in prayer for those now dead.
Symptom of allergies that got fed.
Clouds of dust on paths we had fled.

Eyes of red . . .
Lying awake for hours in bed.
Tossing and turning on what lies just ahead.
Focused on headlines we doth read.
Babe in arms, to care for those we hath bred.

Eyes of red . . .
Quite unbelievable, on something incred!
Stars in the skies with dream's unsaid.
Nauseous cramming for courses in advanced-ed.
Anxious planning jitters when we wed.

You look so tired, your eyes so red.
Trying times, mostly how their fed.
No matter how much you dread.
Bound to be a topic on what is said.
Long before you are dead!

Kevin Randall

"Secrets of Joy"

1) We can find the joy in so many things around us, in many facets of life; 2) From our fairy tale youth times, through to the golden age days. Look for and share your faith in joy; 3) Remember, the best gift is the one you give as a gift!

I wonder if you will ever find me?
    I wonder this aloud.
Then you solve this mystery,
    find one amongst the crowd.
Being together is very endearing;
    loving you is sheer glee to employ.
Almost lost, if we're not nearing,
    is the cost at winning secrets of joy!

Each fabled story of yore is told,
    as we recall from our distance youth.
How the feebled males, at the core, become so bold,
    and the regal princess lives in the truth.
Examples of fray and fright,
    we trace back to samples of our delight:
Jack be nimble, the same one who fell,
    defaced his crown trampled on at the wishing well.

Mary who sat, lost her little lamb,
    yet, grew her garden into such a grand flowery scene.
(Another) Jack, had no fat, yet vined large beans.
    And, Georgey, came to be known as "so lady mean."
'Heroer' David, such a mere man-child,
    dethroned the king of the hill, when he got riled.
Long stories carry on, adhered lessons to employ;
    all lore has grown in thrill to explain the secrets of joy!

The critters of the beast and wild,
    are caught, and can become tame.
That what matters in the least of many child;
    to many a girl and home boy,
Is that we find and flatter in all these beguiled game.
    Woe, can truly shatter the young of heart so coy.
Comic heroes of this era could be labeled such zeros;
    yet, still create today new fabled secrets of joy!

We encounter people of sufferance, in need, and they declare "wanna
    hurt less," in each and every day.
You can make a difference to them with your shared blessings of
    measure in a positive way.
What you hath receive, giveth as a gift, of your time, a talent, a treasure,
    or a festive toy.
You can share your faith, hope, and pleasure; it's dependent how you
    spend such secrets of joy!

"Miss The Call"

1) So many varied vocations in life; 2) Yet, they can have similar end results, if we 'miss' a key important call; 3) Thus, don't be hesitant to exert your "best" positive efforts in completing the tasks at hand. Your contributions can make a BIG difference in reaching an end goal . . . for yourself or for others.

"Miss The Call"

Miss the Call . . .
    The **phone** rang off the wall. Being not near, I couldn't hear at all.
    Was it You?? Didn't see voicemail in view. Did I miss the call?
Refs running down the sidelines in fall. Be so many players, big and small.
Being so mortal. Can't be all that too fatal? See so many plays to call.
Yet, sometimes, too easy to miss the call.
    Soldier Recruitment. Enlistment. Plan for a brawl.
    Helps the USA to always stand tall.
    Depends on your view. Still, it all affects me and you. Proudly, they do not miss the call.
Pastor prayers answered, planned by a Creator. Missions sheltered; acts not so small.
Celebrate Life - Faith as a Leader. God's will, never skeltered at all.
Always focused to not miss the call.
    Civil Service to serve and protect us all. Patrol through city, parks, the mall.
    Safer for us to live. Sharing time, treasure, and life to give.
    Ever so grateful that they never miss the call.
Laborers Weld. Cut. Drive. Mold or Mangle. Many blue-collared jobs for us all.
Helps uplift the economy. They help produce this great country.
Manning shifts to make and reduce, and to not miss the call.

No matter your profession, always do your best. Give it your all.
Make it your mission, work before rest, and don't ever miss the call!

"I Was You"

1) I have experienced mistaken identity; 2) So, admittedly, I went along with the ruse since I o.c. profess to be in some kind of witness protection program; 3) Only to find out later somehow, that it is alright to step to the plate, identify <u>yourself</u> correctly, accept it, and be proud of who you are!

"I Was You"

Yesterday, the telephone did ring,
Didn't want to admit a single thing,
Wouldn't you do the same?
Funny, how I escaped the hurt
I even avoided this call alert
Didn't play the phone game,
Wouldn't you do the same?

Heck, the caller "only needed a ride."
Admit, behind your name I did hide.
Threw him off by the name.
Wouldn't you do the same?

Today, my mind in a better place.
I started to care.
Now, you'd be over there.
Trying a new thing.
Committed, to not be in shame.
If I was you, and you was I??

I just used your name.
Nor, take the blame.
If I was you, and you were I??
By using this small lie.
I was so afraid, way too shy.
Didn't need the fame
If I was you, and you were I??

I still declined; "... I am at work."
What a coward! ". . . I am a jerk!"
In shame, I stood by my fantasy.
If I was you, and you were me??

Wore diff' clothes. Put on a new face.
Bore a new 'spiff' look in the mirror.
How, I'd be right here.
Waiting for the phone to ring.
Wouldn't you do the same?
If I was you, and you was I??

"Wave of Hands"

1) Amazingly, we use the 'wave of hands' in so much of our everyday life. So many differed meanings, at different times; 2) The best use, I declare, is when we share a simple "Hello" wave! 3) Please wave, too! It is such a welcome warming to brighten someone's way! You will feel better, too!

"Wave of Hands"

I see the wave of hands, they mean so much to me.
Most times we understand, it conveys, "Hi" or "Bye," typically.
Other times, to "Thank" someone who let you in line, customarily.
The times missed the most, is when there's "no show of hands," irreverently.
    Why be remiss to demonstrate the "wave the hands", a signal of many meaning?
    Like when you want to go straight, more in reverse, go right or left, or keep y'all from leaning.
    Wave of hands helps apply elbow grease in the act of cleaning.
    Or, a high sign for the thrashing machine to cease, as a fact in the farm fall gleaning.
Concert songs oft bring on wave of hands from the crowd.
Assert or fling of hands to quiet the basement band from rocking too loud.
Flick of a wrist, to erase a sky cloud on a TV forecast.
Or, pump thy fist, to dig up an historic man's face and shroud . . . "to see it at last!"
    Lift' wave of hands, by refs to end each and every play the same.
    Swift wave of hands, mostly fends off any wild critter game.
    We crave Blessed raise hands used to heal the lame in a congregation.
    To the brave, a welcoming wave to get saved when there is a life resuscitation.

Cont.

A solemn wave of hands can be enacted upon the man, "Sir" knighted by Queen and Court.
Or, be a flagged wave sign reacted, that the "discus try" was slightly a bit too short.
Wave sign commotion, a 'self-forgiven plea' at an outward cry, belch, or a loud snort.
Wave of hands motions happen when we accord a happy sigh, or else, in a frenzy sort.

Tisking waves show signs of disgust, or lack of trust.
    Marking waves a target spot to hit, if you must.
    A wave for shooing away those in leer and lust.
    Or, to those too close to the last baked apple pie crust.
Common royal wave, and horn toot, by the County Fair Princess leading a parade.
Solemn loyal wave to honour the Brave in a salute address by the Hero's grave shade.
We can dictate to corral a herd when a wave of hands are made.
    Or, indicate to where the flocks' directions had been made.
    Or, to wave for your pet to get closer to be played.
Basically, a wave of hands is a habit in every rendezvous.
Dramatically, thanking those we praise, to get to stand.
Traumatically, wave to those who went askew.
Ultimately, a wave of hands ripple is grand to those in our near view.
Mainly, I always look for the simple "Hello" command wave of hands
    from you!
A wave of hands is a "Hi" sign out loud,
So, wave those hands, and be proud!

"Rush of Time"

1) Life is short, making time as a dual-edged sword, because we want time to fly in the anticipation of a happy, big event; however, when we're in the event 'attendance,' we want time to go slower to savor the glad moments; 2) Being a songwriter "wannabe," I developed a rhythm in this prose for a special family time; 3) Humming along to happy tunes in the drive, added to the fun "Q" Time during the visit! Happy Trails to You! March On! Sing On!

It's been 24, Time sure seems to fly.

My waiting has been one big blur. C'mon clock, don't die!

Case in point, as family, we chatted 'bout the weather, then made plans to meet.

Our road course was duly platted. We'll finally be together, How sweet!

> Pushed for the mid-point to be our site. Saturday noon, our rendezvous date.
>
> Rushed, we cleared our joint dockets, to my delight. Eager to drive . . . just can't be late!
>
> Time awaits for no one; yet, with bursting impatience, I am overly filled.
>
> Gosh! Am looking forward to my son's fun-thirsting presence. I am truly thrilled!

Finally, the appointed day had arrived. Had 'over' readied for my leg of trip.

Really don't know how I survived. Had studied maps, ya, ya, ya . . . No getting lost, I just can't slip.

Cont.

All week, watched the clock seem mired. Funny, Ha! Ha! Ha! How Father Time, now seems to flip.
Just when spirits are most afire, NOW, is when I don't want to race time. My Heart takes a dip.
    Gotta just fight the urge to glance at the clock on the wall.
    Senses been building up at every chance, you know, me meeting my son, and all.
    Today, the date is here, like primping for a grand dance or ball.
        I'm begging the sweeping hands to stall.
Packed car and me start out fast to cover the miles distance.
        I'm wishing the weekend time to crawl . . . Time being my resistance.

Havin' one full weekend to ourselves. At the shore; this road trip to repeat some history.
Even tho' we made these treks before, we await to make a new memory.
Passing trucks, out in the fast lane. Pedal to the floor. Heading down Highway 43.
Near noon has struck, adrenalin in my vein. Shuttle off once more, 'cause "That's my Baby!"

    His pictures on my dash, by the signal . . . er, maybe somewhat irrational.
    Inspires me to motor like a flash, past signs, ramps, even the mall.
    Doesn't matter that my wind draft flings trash in my rear directional.
    Checked my wallet for some cash; and, yes, peeked at the clock, so motivational!

Dreamin' big of what we'll do. Since our 'together' time is so far between and so few.
Screamin' past each road reflector post. My son doesn't matter which one of us plays the host.
Go South. East. West. Up Nort'. We trade trips planned of varied assort.
This time: neutral court. By the shore, to admire sailing ships . . . amazing time to not fall short.

My mind now snaps to my driving chore, as my exit is in view.
    Yes! Beat those speed traps to the shore, good thing there were only a few.
    Just minutes away . . . I beat my record time score. Soon, "by noon," I'll be in blissful glee.

"Hey! There's my son for real," I chime. Did I tell ya before, "He's my son?" "That's my baby!"
"Yes, that's my baby!" Every time I see him, I just gush!
And, wouldn't you know it, if you will, right this minute, Time stands still! Oh! What a rush!

Kevin Randall

"Holloween Haunting Horror"

1) One of America's great seasonal tradition is chaperoning the children on a haunted house tour, which I try to bravely survive by telling myself, "It's for the kids!" 2) On a "former" friend's dare, I tried to overcome my "hate allergy" for this scary ritual, but still could not stomach the haunting horror experiences, which parallels my total dislike for other national staples, like mac 'n' cheese, certain veggies, and the color pink, "Ugh!"
3) As un-American as my selective allergies are, I gave one more haunted house trip the good All-American try! Read on how that went.

'Tis the season of Halloween, my two kids begged for a "Trick or Treat" scary scene.
No reason to be mean, Friday the 13th, was pegged to be our early Halloween.
Yes, an ad for a haunted house said "they would be open for all of October."
So, we dressed as "Scaredy-Cat," "Timid Mouse," and "Bad-Man Fred," as I remember.

Us three, conjured happy thoughts, as we took our place in line with goblins, ghouls, and ghosts.
Endured sappy shouts, while I looked at a sign: "Come in - if you dare! We'll scare ya' the most!"
I gulped, hesitated . . . and being spooked, slowly shuffled to enter.

Cont.

My kids whooped, ne'er waited; pulled and muffled, me, in their center.
At the dimly lit porch steps, we're met by a blast of air, then an eerie, whispering "boooooo . . ."
My eyes barely seeing in this darkened set; "buyer beware," . . . Who got me into this anywhoo??
Knuckle clenching, fumbling along the first wall, as I recall, steered to a trapped door.
Buckled, flinching, stumbling, to a witches call; snapped, sneered, "Can't you take this anymore?"

Yet, we stopped, pushed the squeaky door, only to see, like a small red light. This set was so cooped, a sneaky corpse on the floor. Yikes! I was a ball of fright!

Then a strobing bus globe was found around the corner.
Hands protruding at us; profound sounds of screaming terror.
Swift, a stabbing dagger, reached through caged bars.
Lift, my sobbing eyes, I staggered, screeched, "How'd we ever get this far?"

In the next terrorred scene, a flying hag on her broom, "Come with me, to the stairs!"
She cackled horridly mean. Me crying, "Ugh!" Off she vroomed, dumb, how much this scares!
Trying to recover, we crept along to see one dead bloom on a tomb of fright.
A lone undertaker, wept in song, "You're next to doom!" My stomach churned so tight.
This widow-maker pried open a coffin of wood; all blood, guts, terror, and gore!
I was the sad slacker, cried, if I could. A real pud. More scared than ever before!

In this maze, pulled along by "boooos!" from my kids, when out flashed a wild hairy creature!
Truly dazed! Dulled, my shoes hit the skids! Or, I'd have crashed right into that scary feature!
The hair on my own head, tho' few, raised to a new doomed level.
Aware, "I'm not dead yet?" True! I appraised; yet, my own costume so disheveled.

Then to our total shock, we gasped . . . as we reached the next room cell.
When we mortally stopped from our brutal walk at what we grasped . . . a pure gloom of hell!
Although this reduced space was the smallest of them all,
It produced what we faced, the biggest detested nightmare from its wall!

How, sick was the one who made this scene caper sight?
Now, this trick made us all shade our eyes from this "paper" fright!
No flying witches, no rabid bats, no stalking zombies stink, nor talking dead . . .
No crying ghosts, no black cats, but shocking "pink wall paper," instead!

So, with all our fury, and all our might, we blasted thru walls and doors, past a barrel 'a-burn'.
"GO! GO!" we scurried that fright night! So we forecasted, "NEVER MORE!" Never to Return!

Moral of this wicked story, tale of fright and gory detail:
    In the season of "Trick or Treat" scary things,
      The worst 'trick' is to see how "pink wall paper" stings,
        'Cause the nightmares it forever brings!

Kevin Randall

"Knock On Wood"

1) Had the "winter cabin fever" blues; 2) Tried all sorts of remedies; 3) Best cure? Having a dear friend's timely superstitious "knock on wood" at my door! Such an endearing sentiment, that was spot-on timely, and preciously priceless!

Just another hazy, winter sleeting, 'bluesy' afternoon. Then, you knocked faintly on my door.
"Welcome!" was my greeting. "Glad to see ya' so soon. Too bad you hadn't called on me before!"
My thoughts had cluttered, sauntered. Lost, I shuttered in, hoping on an early spring.
My words barely muttered, so self-centered. My gaze ne'er wandered, past your eyes of serene green.
    Now it hit me! That, *I* was the one who had called you! To such a friend so true!
    Directly, you hastened to my door. Dashing, you did not falter.
    Ne'er questioned me of the score, nor rushing to, "What's *really* the matter?"

You entered. The tension and attention, on me, it clearly centered. Your calming aura catered, mentioned "I'll ever be there." Such calming eyes, how sweet to see!

Eased my mind. You took the time. So nice to have a friend that cared. Time well shared.
    You became the mirror I needed. Your advice well heeded.
    Just your presence was beyond belief. Soft green eyes brought such fond relief!
Spent. My senses had been shot. Overfilled with blues. Overfed against the winter chills.
Vented, "Them blues is what I got!" Numb, I felt dead. My thinking had gone still.
You listened true. And, a lot! Yet, you did not push, nor overkill.
Wow! My troubles were vacated. All disappeared. Lightened my load.
How time doubles as our enemy. Placated on what I feared, you buttoned up to hit the winter road.
YES! I'd say, you sure helped erase those 'cabin blues'; gotten me through by the caring eyes that you bode.

You couldn't stay, I understood. Now my mood so happy, I warmly embraced you once more, as I should.
Brightened me up from the way I first stood; I'm so lucky you engaged my door with a "knock on wood!"

Kevin Randall

"Magic Wand Spell"

1) How a band in motion can cause such emotion! 2) Like, how different genres of music can take us back to long-ago memories, as elementary as A-B-C; 3) All initiated thru a magic wand, that carries such spell bounding power as a big stick! Tap! Tap! Tap!

"Ahem! Ummm . . . Quiet please in the room."
All eyes on The Magic Wand, raised in silence, the Conductor lowers it soon.
Funny, how a simple baton wand can arouse the big band!
Tap – Tap – Tap, to attention, the hush suddenly resumes.
All ears now await for the next magic wand spell sleight of hand.
And with a simple wave, a few piercing notes, before the drums boom, to fill this silence in the room.
The crowd is under a spell. It is simple as A-B-C, to the audience's delight what the ears do consume.
A-B-C, hear what "The Magic Wand" can create just by its symbol!
  A- For the "Amen" hymn a humming, we remember so well,
  B- For the "Be in love" serenade melody that two can surely tell,
  C- For the Classic Symphony, that make every emotions swell!

A-B-C, we Alone, the Band, the Crowd, All under "The Magic Wand" mesmerizing spell!

  A- Is for the Alto sax, a sounding out a few notes,
  B- Brass slowly joining in its brash blues quotes,
  C- Clarinet reeds do add some class that truly floats.

A-B-C, A- A simple hymn we learned in Sunday Class,
    B- Beat and tempo added to any string key splash,
    C- Cymbals come together to clash n' crash!

A-B-C, A single horn belting out select notes we recall so well!
All brought on by The Magic Wand," and that agile sleight of hand.
As soon as we hear it, our memories can name that tune, a loving afternoon,
Our minds can wander back to yesteryear, remember dear? Pray tell!
All brought on by A-B-C music, that stirs the soul, like a dance floor stroll.

> A- That simple hymn we recall; an Almighty psalm played for us all.
> B- 'Be in love' serenade, a blast from the past, that makes our memories last.
> C- Combined all orchestra sections to our heart and soul delight!
> How they play with all their might!

All brought on by the "Magic Wand Spell," and the sleight of hand!
That joy stick kick-stands the band, and resounding notes again.
Beat those drums, bring on the brass that string along the beat.
Sexy sax notes heat up the ivory keys in such harmony duet, to hold us in our seat.
Serenade to take flight, to carry us through the late night.
Can those simple notes ever begin so slowly, yet cloud the room so glowingly?
Clarinets add some class, clash of cymbals in this concerto, can create such a stir enjoyingly!

A-B-C, all combined in one big joining of band, the hand, and "The Magic Wand"
Sir O'Maestro, play it all again! Encore, from a symphony long ago!
Play as planned in crescendo, to fill our hearts and souls so!
The crowd hanging on every key; in result, of the matter and the music chatter of A-B-C,
The wowed magic flutter of the Wand spell over the band, all played for you and me!

Kevin Randall

"Don Those Shoes"

1) The proverbial saying, "Is the grass greener on the other side?" 2) Lessons to be learned by all generations . . . and that is so illustrated by grandchildren-age drawing a pair of anyone's shoes! 3) Yes, children can teach us adults to grow and show empathy for other people by their naïve innocence of understanding others who are not as fortunate in life as others. Thus, us adults, we must keep the faith in the next generation, and be proud of walking in our own shoes, and where they take us . . .

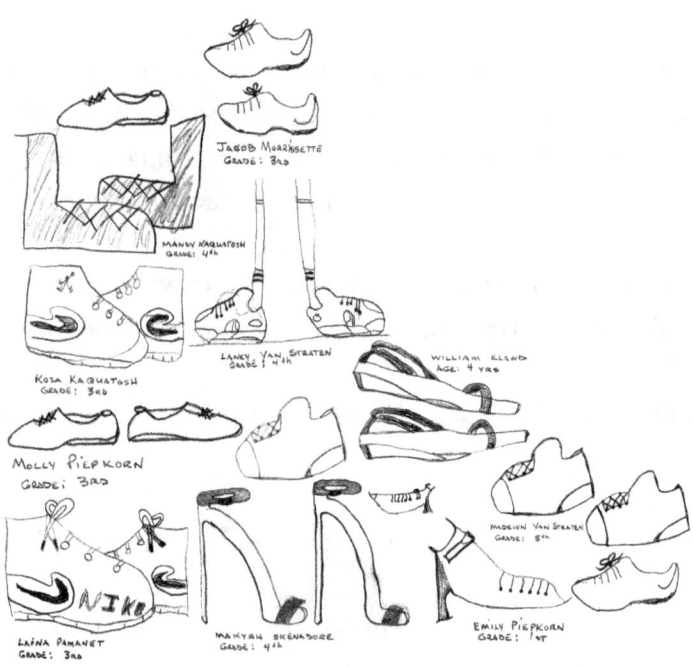

Just Three Words

"Don Those Shoes"

You think that you got it rough? Some days go so well, others are pure hell and tough.
So you complain and pout. Wanna not answer the bell, but just yell out with a shout.
You say, "I just hate . . . ! How come life's so hard for me?" So, please wait, let's check reality.

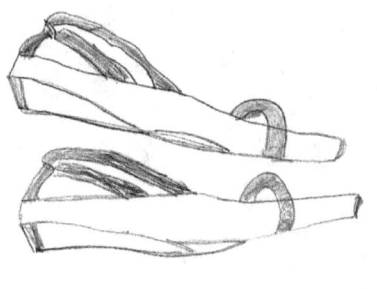

WILLIAM ELAND
AGE: 4 YRS

You look upon others who seem to have it easy, "Why can't I be like that?" you say. From where you stand and walk, you feel there is "no good luck about to land, any day."
I say, let's change that talk today. And try to understand, how another might view their way.

Yes, don their shoes onto <u>you</u>!
Big or small, you place your toes in their shoes. You choose.
Look from "the other side" to choose the other guys walk.
Through it all, you have to swallow your own pride, not lose to your own "down" talk.
Thru the blues and thru the pain you have to retrain your steps to their stride.

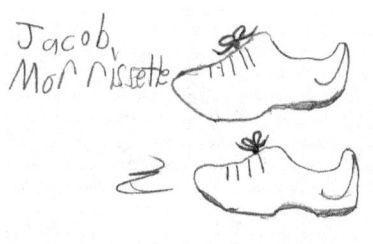

JACOB MORRISSETTE
GRADE: 3RD

Cont.

LAINA PAMANET
GRADE: 3RD

One step, then again . . . refrain from any complain, take steps to be on" their side." Heels or laced, no matter where their placed, walk in their shoes, with care and pride.

Thus, don their shoes!

You think, "The grass is a touch mere greener?" when on the other side.

Or, that your world amass is so much more meaner? So, let's peer closer, before you decide.

The deck is stacked against you. You feel you are deemed "a loser" in <u>your</u> narrowed eyes.

All, until you take a closer view, it just seems only that

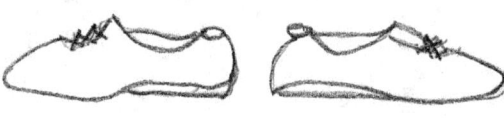

MOLLY PIEPKORN
GRADE: 3RD

<u>you</u> are one being heralded as despised.

Once you dissect the situation, you find, the only hate is not by others, only by you.

Man, you came to a brash conclusion. But, you can overcome any rash illusion,

KOSA KAQUATOSH
GRADE: 3RD

when you "walk the talk" in the other guys shoes, too. Thus, don those shoes!

Wear them to turn the mental tide. Don those shoes, and go pace in their stride.

You can chose to slip on sandals, or lace up those extra-wides; go face it, swallow your own pride.

See the world as a brand new global person, focus on the new local view inside with good reason.

Just Three Words

Yes, the stories they tell, maybe worse than your very own.
Guess their glories aren't so well, in their purse and verse, they ever do bemoan.
It takes some gumption and doing, so trust me, take a reverse, and go see clearer as they do.
Altho' there are assumptions on-going, you must step nearer into a different view.

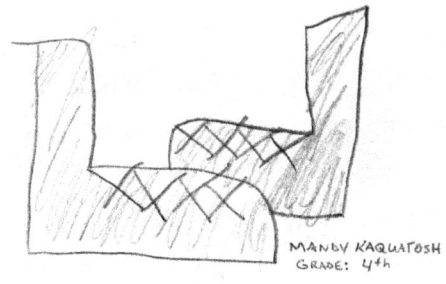

MANDY KAQUATOSH
GRADE: 4th

LANEY VAN STRATEN
GRADE: 4th

Thus, those shoes that you do don, wear them well; swallow your pride.
Don those shoes, and not wallow with defeat inside.
Big or small, the shoes in which they are worn to walk, don't always fit everyone.
Blisters and sores beget thru the shear pain. Thru it all, chose to "walk the talk," not to complain.

Resist to just sit and say, "My life's just not fun."
Apathy? Have you been wearing blinders about others and their ways, and not seen how they made it thru?
Empathy! Begin caring on what bad opinions hinders, remove those sad binders that smothers,
and step into a new view: "Theirs" versus "what you choose;"
Thus, don those shoes.

MADELYN VAN STRATEN
GRADE: 5th

Cont.

Kevin Randall

See the world contrasted in how you had previously eyed.
Take a twirl, not time wasted, on how to feel when <u>their</u> pairs are obviously tied.
    Loafer, tennies. Heeled, or not, the style is moot.
    Floaters and pennies. Steeled, or pigskin leather boots.

No matter the size or style, walk a mile in the other guys stride.
Ego and toes may shatter, but now you can talk with a difference inside.
Don those shoes, the ones that you select to choose, and feel the other guy's muse.
Now, don those shoes, your own suedes, browns or blues. Walk and talk, with renewed self-pride!

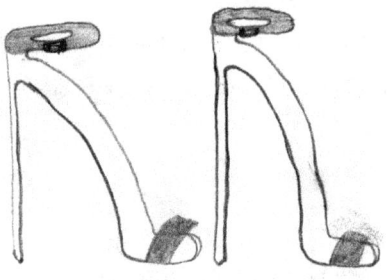

Don those shoes to have a new life view. From now on, walk with pride as a new YOU, in your own shoe!

" 'Closer' Versus 'Loser' "

1) We all have choices to make; 2) The level of consequences/ results can depend upon a person's vocation/situation in life, or in that instant; 3) Remember, the harder the course, more rewarding the triumph!

You are on a walk, thinking you should "race her."
You know, the lady that just jogged by.
In your 'internal talk,' could you "face her"?
Others would say, "Hey, Loser. Just go try!"

> You study hard to be a doctor.
> Maybe a lawyer, learner, fireman, plumber.
> You strategize to pass the test to become such a prime "Closer."
> Otherwise, your friends will then call you that "all-time Loser!"

You aim to prove you can do right, that you can be something good.
Study with drive and might, and become what you should.
You desire to what they say, that you became a real 'go-getter'.
So, be the "Closer" versus "Loser."

> Babe. Child. Teen. Woman.
> You have grown up, the best you can.
> Poise, posture, that's the way, your parents "raised her," as others would say.
> You keep hearing that chant in your head: "I'm a Closer! Ain't no Loser!"

You are pointed right. Couldn't be more surer!
Prove it to their sight. Be the "Closer!" not the "Loser!"
To what they say, doesn't matter. It's you that has to decide.
So, you go pick a side: "Closer!" versus "Loser!"

"There Once Was"

1) 9/11 changed all of America, and the world's air transportation significantly; since pre-9/11, many of us travelers took 'flying free of evil threat' for granted; like hearing the 'sound of freedom' in the flights overhead; 2) Then, during the 9/11 phase, all subsequent flights were suspended, leaving us to bear the deafening silence in the skies; 3) Hereafter 9/11, through prudent safety measures enacted, we in America can now once again hear the (plane) sounds of freedom in our friendly skies, which is our constant reminder to be aware of our safety surroundings. Proudly Fly On, USA!

THERE ONCE WAS . . . (pre-9/11)

A plane to fly so free
> above this very land.

Just as we see the eagle be
> floating, soaring, above the sea and sand.

With clarity, we heard the engine roaring,
> boasting for the plane to fly free.

Our sincerity, to Fly Free! Simply. Naturally.

THERE ONCE WAS . . . (during 9/11)

An evil plot in history
> that changed the course of time.

Made some flights full of misery;
> how damaged and savaged the remorse in our mind.

Once again, we awaited every plane sounding, or any?
> To regain our dignity as a country so kind.

Our gallantry, to Fly Free! Diligently. Respectfully.

Just Three Words

THERE ONCE WAS . . . (post-9/11)
A huge part of the comeback plan,
       to regain our friendly sky.
We just had to take a stand,
       and rebound, for each plane to fly.
Once again, we aimed for flying to be fun adventures
       and longed for passing smiles.
We retained to return our flight junctures;
       we came back stronger to higher, safer-lasting miles.
Our goal shared heroically, to Fly Free! Motivationally. Customarily.

THERE ONCE WAS . . . (today: 'lest not us forget 9/11)
How we proceeded, was in one united front,
       to fly through all types of weather.
Oh, believe me, we succeeded, in this hunt!
       We made it through together!
Once again, we pack your bags to fly,
       steered to a high view so much better.
We are now back, to soar safe and high,
       cleared for takeoff, today, as real go-getters.
Today, we are proud and dared, to Fly Free! Inspirationally. Patriotically!

Kevin Randall

"Some Midpoint View"

1) Taking sides is not always the preferred P.C. course of action; i.e., maybe not an appropriate thing to do in family matters; 2) Yet, two-sided issues can be a good thing in causing us to choose a view in a reasonable debate; 3) So go choose a side, for a noble cause and remember, you are the one who has to live with that decision.

The topping is so appealing
>	the crust we crave, full of spice.

The middle filling is left untouched,
>	a must to save, "Ah! It's so nice!"

The earth is green and so full;
>	the sky, true blue and light;

We're in the mid-point lull,
>	yet, loving that hue just right!

Sprouts grow up 'neath us,
>	as rays dribble upon us from above,

Trees abound around us,
>	we stay in the middle, where Man surrounds us with His love.
>	The midpoint is the Mind, between our Hearts of giving and our
>	>	Souls of living.
>	The "mid" is the 'soft-find' within the tough shell;

We, at times, caught weaving our senses of mind between Heaven and Hell.

Many midpoints out there . . . here is a few more to share . . .
    As we pause to ponder,
        is the rhyme for no reason or with a cause?
    Songs instill us to chime in, no wonder,
        before another note of time, or breath of pause.
    Music is the magic in the middle,
        a language heard by all.
    "Beginners," "enders," "mid-extenders,"
        anguish over that, "all join in to sing!" at the beckoned call.

Poems, the prose with a "drum beat" of truth.
    Thru the years we remember those, "the songs so sweet," 'lest we forget our youth.
    The "mid" is the real meaning part, between the meter heard, and the tapping of the feet.
    The second stanza found on the stage set, between the first act and third feat.
    Where the crescendo gives its best increasing tempo heard beat!

You see, there are many cases, where it is all right to be caught on neither one side nor two.
It is a safe haven that traces us back to be taught by another's "midpoint view."

Kevin Randall

"Respect Her Privacy"

1) Coming of age gives the youth an inherent right to earn their respectful privacy; 2) Especially, this holds true in safeguarding her diary writs, a sacred place in her heart, and we should keep it that way. 3) During her formative pre-teen and teenager years, give her good, solid fundamental valued parental guidance, and chances are she will respect your wishes on selecting 'good' life choices in return.

From a babe to a young girl, a grown teen prints in her diary.
We know things to "never see," so we keep to ourselves and respect her privacy.
     As she matures, to keep her space as she wishes, we do not taunt.
     Small in statures, the best places she relishes, we do not haunt.
     Allow her that room as we would want,
     Girls' mind, body, soul, we shall not flaunt.
     Coming of age, (within reason), we let her be, we respect her privacy.
Give her the sole time to refresh and put on her "day face."
Grant her 'logic' freedom, and let her mesh with <u>your</u> time and space.
Honour the kingdom code of a closed door base.

She has earned her keep, hopefully,
Awake and asleep, we respect her privacy.
>   Hearing her whispers and secrets, we keep inside.
>   Bearing her respect with no regrets, with her heart she can confide.
>   Let her bloom, then thru time, lets her smile that we had even tried.

Mind to mind. Heart to heart. Soul to soul, reverently. We respect her privacy.

Together, she has our understanding, making right choices to be her responsibility.

Others may want to break her privacy landing, speaking in wrong voices, we expect her own 'voting' ability.

Out in the world she is her own person. We raised and praised her to be one in sound reason.

We all breathe easier she lived rightfully, thus, we remain bound to respect her privacy.

>   We don't bug her phone, nor block her text, nor 'friends.'
>   She has to choose on her own, to deter and not mock, "what's next?"
>   at each of our visit ends.

She has the right to speak freely; so, we continue to live in a "give and take" world habitually.

A grand woman she has grown up to be! Must have a lot to do, that we always respected her privacy.

"Three Times Soliloquy"

1) First-ever written prose of substance to reveal my teen years of moodiness and finding my way in life; 2) And, to be understood, as I limped along at the beat of my own drum; 3) Being my own independent thinker was hard, so to fit in I used some comically, wry wit and humour which can be labeled as my own "kevinisms" . . . See if you can find those words scattered throughout this literary piece, as well as others in this entire book.

>... 1st-, as I wrote it . . .
>
>.. 2nd, as you heard it . . .
>
>...3rd, as it was meant to be . . .

It's foolish. We're so close, yet so far.

We see each other about every day; but do we?

When we do speak, the words aren't there, yet the eyes have it.

> It's foolish. I've yet to communicate, although you have initiated my mind,
>
> Opened my heart;   however, we both know that blocks still do exist.

It's so foolish, to be out of bounds this way, and still be in the game.

Why is it that hope lingers, when so many answers are still untold to questions unasked?

> Be kind now. It's all new to me, but played before. It's foolish, I'm still a beginner.
>
> To follow in thee's footsteps is no easy task. I may ask for too much by not asking?

It's foolish. Be slow to help me grow.

Solitude is nice. Pleasure you give is fantastic. Happiness is the end Joy. Deep inside, desire just feelings enjoyed by many others. That's all that I ask, too.

> It's foolish. I actually open up to you more than I should.
>
> Out of bounds? Probably more than you would.
>
> The touch of reality sets in.

A sense of realism emoted. That's why a dreamer goes on – to live, now. In the now.

To try what he can't. Bring back what he shan't.

> Efforts put forth before, not hereafter, may be looked upon as foolish.
>
> Only a fool would say . . . ?" Aw, so, go be a fool!

". . .If I forget the way, the running river, the quiet green, still someday, just once, let the wind blow through me, let me breathe free . . ."

~ ANON

Kevin Randall

"My Backyard Swing"

1) My own kid's days had this delightful memory of a backyard swing; 2) A very vivid peek into the special swing enshrined at Grandpa & Grandma's house at Gravel Hill Farm; 3) And although our 'together' times were limited, it was the best of times for a kid's eternal joy!

"My Backyard Swing"

All of us kids recall the 'special trip spot' when we were just 'a wee real tot.'

How we'd all jump for joy, "Ship off to Grandpa and Grandma's house! Oh! Boy!"

Grandma in her fixin' apron, stokin' the baking oven, or yolking and mixing the puddin' pie.

Grandpa came in from the field, taking time to yield, just to sit a spell relaxing, and lettin' time go fly.

As we drove up the Gravel Hill Farm lane, my sisters and I would strain, an eye out for our favorite thing.

We craned our necks to get a peek at that treasure. To yell out, the first to speak, "My Backyard Swing!"

Delighted by Grandma's hugs, kisses on cheeks, and "tickled bugs" for good measure; all, at her torn door.

Ah! Grandma Nina's old-style kitchen, to smell her cookin'; what was smokin', sweet aromas you couldn't ignore!

After our bold smiled "Hellos!" when we got in, we followed our 'freckled, pug-lookin' noses, and ran out the slamming screen door.

We pushed open the gate, rushed in since we couldn't wait, to meet Grandpa, who might have been a'snore.

Yelled to him, "Grandpa Hugh !" sitting as a royal king, from his wooden throne view, the regal Backyard Swing!

Being first to reach him, mind ya', meant you got to sit next to him, the prized seat, (next to our "king!")

Cont.

He awoke so spry, to hear our greeting cry, in that late July's heat, far from spring!
"Ha! Ha!" We then got to do, so tickled of what we craved . . . "Why, just our most favorite thing!"
Grandpa handed us a dime or nickel he had saved, as we jumped with delight upon the Backyard Swing!
When he asked us, "Will you be good?" Of course, we nodded "we would,"
    as we slowly started to fling.
Then, as we basked in our ride, we had spied, a pesky horsefly on him. Worse, without being prodded,
    he then retorted 'bout his latest bee sting.
On our ride, we also saw a rabbit a'run, squirrels up a tree, and flowers' full bloom that July.

(A quick aside to take you away from our long-ago history 'happy high':
What made that year so rare, as we look back, Grandpa's last summer before he would die.
"No time to spare" as we kept track, losing him, a past "bummer,"
so the swinging felt so good to our core, sitting next to him that July!)

Now, back to our happy yesterday story, when we were in such kid glory, just doing our favorite thing.
Oh, we would fight so, as siblings might go, bragging, "It's <u>MY</u> Backyard Swing!"
Grandpa would "halt," to "stop" this fault, as he reached for his shaker of salt, stashed on the swing arm.

Just Three Words

Handed us all a treat, swinging on our seat, "TOE-MAE-TOES!" to eat, ripened in summer heat, splashed in childhood charm!
Fresh from the vine, no time to lose, handed out one to choose; with our sleeves we made them shine.
Upon each salted bite, to our exalted delight, we ALL claimed that, "the biggest, was Mine!"
Our next swinging ritual, so easy to be on a winging habitual, we all got into our bare feet.
To try to feel the cool residual grass, at each swinging futile pass – all, from our happy wooden seat.
Funny, how we kept sync in gelled time, as the squirrels would tree-climb, to our "counting out" tempo beat.
Granny, then yelled out as our linked-swing so swirled, "Clean-up! Don't drop your dime. It's time to eat!"

"Okay, ya'!" We tried real hard to squeeze in a few more minutes of sway, to keep our spirits up to soar.
Grandpa, left the yard with his cane, in a wheeze; so, as any "kids at play" do, we then tried to make each sweep roar s'more.

Today, we as kids, reminisced the end of each farm dust trip, as we departed down the Gravel Hill Farm lane.
Say, we all "kissed and missed" our Grandma, with her pie crust crimp, and Grandpa with his "TOE-MAE-TOES" thrill, and worn cane.
Yes! We miss, too, the best stories long ago of our childhood favorite thing.
Guess, to test our memories, 'Viola'! Sitting with Grandpa in flight, on "My Backyard Swing!"

Kevin Randall

"Give Me Three"

1) My mantra in writing customized prose is that I ask for "just three words;" 2) Then the writing challenge is so much more fun, since it does afford me a chance to stretch my writing talent, as limited as it is, and complete a customized piece to share the end results as a gift; 3) Ultimately, the proof is in the end result, like whenever I receive the favorable targeted, "I like it" feedback response from the recipient! Thanks to all who have contributed their three words, AND, being so dang truthful whether you even liked the poem or not!

I came to you yesterday, asking for, "just three words" you'd say.
That, "I'll make a poem some way."
First, you think it will be short piece, not a daring essay.
"You see, while others are at work, I am writing at play."
All in "just three words," that you came to say.
> Text, I took the "just three words" that you wrote down in original measure.
> Perplexed, I developed them to my thinking, and for your personal pleasure.
> Next, composed your words into hopes that you'd eternal treasure.

So, I was off writing in a frantic fray,
Like a plighting lunatic in dismay.
To befit you, as my greatest critic, about my prose today.
With hopes that you enjoyed the "just three words" composed gem some way.

    I know that some of it, won't be 'a hit.'
    That for some bit, you may not 'even give a s…!"
    In the end, I hope that poem mainly meets your, "I get it!"
Now, I just hope to hear that it is a hit. Your poem, as you assay.
Then, I can come back to ask for "just three words," again some other day.
    Tell a prose tale; see how the words do fit.
    Hear you say, "just three words;" and "How they've grown quite a bit!"
    "Sure took longer than a New York minute! "Glad my poem left you in the right spirit!"

Didn't ask for money on a silver tray. Or, just waiting on what you had to say.
While others are at work, I am at play. Hoping that my poetic message has something of value to say.
All styled from, "just three words," that you had first managed to say!

"Big Girl Hat!"

1) Sighted a pre-school, naïve 4-K girl at the "Lie-berry"! What drew my attention, as well as other patrons' attention that afternoon, was this little girl standing in the middle of the "Lie-berry" thoroughfare adorned by her "Big Hat"! Reading aloud at times, from her oversized book. 2) Made my mind jump right to the adult conclusion that this girl was living her "fairy tale dream" in real "present day" time; 3) And why shouldn't she? Since our own youthful tales usually disappear way too quickly . . . Dream On, Big Girl!

> I saw her at the "Lie-berry," standing next to her "shopping," waiting Mom.
> If looks could kill (and they will!), she will always be hoping, dating, for the Prom.
> Well, it's a little girl, bearing a ponytail curl, wearing a "Big Girl Hat!"

With huge book in hand, the words she doesn't understand, but a tale she knows so well.

Mind in a swirl, lost in a "fairy tale world," peering on where's she's "at." That's the little girl, wearing little girl hair twirls, under the "Big Girl Hat!"

With flowers on her hat band, think she's in a Make-Believe-Land, I couldn't really tell?

Her spellbound tale fantasy within, all to see was her smiling grin, the charm of this l'il Southern Belle.

> Her eyes hidden from view, shoelaces tied times two, I then saw what looked like a frown.
> Dropped her lower face chin, her head was aswim, wrapped up in a picture story town.

> It's a little girl face, shirt full of silvery lace, imagining her in a fairy tale grown-up gown!
>
> She kept reading at her pace, in this "Lie-berry" place; pondering, she sat down.

I just knew that she felt at home, reading that book on her own, wearing that "Big Girl Hat!"

Then, heard her moan, fearing that story line "all alone," she said aloud, "Where am I at?"

Then she looked around, another smile to erase that frown, and cried out "Mommy!"

Not able to put that book down, nor dazed by the "Big Girl Hat" crown, she pointed wide-eyed, "It's me!"

> If you peered over her shoulder, she became much bolder, "living in" the book at hand.
>
> The pictures seemed to mold her, as the floor got much colder, she stood up to take a stand.

All the words she couldn't read, pictures helped her memory to feed, that she was the story part "dolly!"

An adult reader she didn't need. Yes, pictures planted that seed! To "say" the story by heart, by golly.

Why, she's the little girl, wearing little girl hair, wearing the "Big Girl Hat!"

Caught up in her own world, without any ol' care, reading the book is where she's "at!"

Found out, the book tale was 'bout a girl of fame who had a dolly the same, she thought she was "that!"

It's a little girl in the "Lie-berry," standing next to Mommy Deary; yet, she imagined she lived in a far off land.

Little girl, extra-ordinary, caught up in this tale of fairy, now a "Big Hat Girl," with huge book in hand!

Kevin Randall

"Gang's All Here"

1) On a summer Friday evening, I was strolling the resort boardwalk out on Main Street, and from the sidewalk, heard such marvelous tunes emitting from within one establishment. 2) True story, I was instantly drawn in to see not a single other patron in sight, yet the band played on as tho' it was a concert for hundreds! 3) Ah, the awesome music and great vocals, plus our personal bantering, made that night so special, entertaining for my personal muse! And the band played on . . . and to think, for that particular night, that I made "The Gang" complete!

"Gang's All Here"

"Molly and the Gang" played roarin' music, heard from the walk.
Slowly entered thru "The Still" bar door mosaic, to see the band leered and gawk.
Not another soul in the place, those within were found full of shock.
To see at least one fan there, "Me!" To play to by face and grin, and to mull and talk.

   I looked around, and indeed, saw no one else at the bar.
   "Come in!" Molly hailed me down. "Tonite, Boss, you're the Star!"
   "Yeah, Man!" echoed a band member, tightening his guitar.
   "We may not play a lot of numbers. Hope you didn't come far?"
"The Gang" stroked out another song, to welcome me so specially!
I spoke at the end, to her Band throng, thanking them, "Well, you see, it's my birthday!"
They stopped. Then played some more. Molly flanking them, broke in, "Reeaallly?"
Then, at the next music break, I evoked, "Nah, You just make me feel that way!"

   They poured me an ale, and I just sat back to hear her hum and sing.
   All "The Gang," being male, nodded during their track, while Molly strummed on the strings!
   I rejoiced, before I was to bail, while one made a crack from his drummer's offerings.
   Molly toasted a wail, "Happy Birthday, to the King, Sir Mack, and whatever this summer night brings!"
I truly felt like a king, as "The Still" music rang! They played just to me, "The Gang," my royal court!

Cont.

Molly sang like a queen, while "The Gang" portrayed as her truly back-up regal support.

"The Gang," as was seen, joined in and all sang at the chorus track. Then, she stopped them so short.

"I get it! Bet you're one of those secret agents, dropping by to talk smack, for a music critic report?"

I gulped my beer, to pretend the beer didn't go down, to go along with the joke.

"Oh, didn't think it was that clear? Gee, I'm found out before I even spoke!"

"Yeah, I came from afar. Heard the news of Molly and The Gang . . . "All ye' band folk."

"Just driving in my car on cruise, by golly. Just to hang at "The Still," for the fan news to be broke."

"Well let's play a tune then, just for you . . . again! WOW! To earn that rave review."

"Who knows, with some good PR, we should be rich by June end! NOW, all the pressures on you!

They "bribed" me with another drink from the bar that spilled over the schooner. "That should do!"

I jived to their next set, that got me to think, "Molly is the best crooner!" while I headed to the loo.

Upon my return to the barstool, Molly blared out, "Hey! Mr. Undercover, bet, you're from the Big City!"

Played along like a fool, "Nah, the next town over. By the way, before another set, got change for a twenty?"

"Well, boys we been taken to school. Played our hearts out, just for this clown rover! Such a pity!"

"Heard your music sound so cool from the street," I relayed. "I drove down and o'er to hear YOU, Molly!"
> She happily, slappily kidded back, "The real band hits the stage at ten!"
> Me, not taking any fiddler flack, "I guess then, maybe I should sit here 'til then?"
> "Oh, Geez! It's your birthday, so we can fill-in if you got a dime to spend."
> "I will stay, please, to hear more that you'll play at 'The Still.' Yes, I have time to lend."

They finished up so upbeat, while I took another long sip.
The band played so sweet, like the notes from songster Molly's lip.
"Thanks for the special B-Day treat! I better get going to my car for my return trip."
"Next year, we'll have a full house seat! The Rave newsletter bit better be 5-Star!" was her stern quip.
"I am one inspired fan in the Up Nort land tonight," as I toasted them with my last beer.
"Lucky to have walked into 'The Still' just on their echo sound, not on sight," I boasted to them so clear.
Molly sang, talked, made my Happy Birthday 'fan solo' a thrill! All found on this night self-roasted premiere.
Then Molly and the entire band retired for the night to my "Gotta Go!" cheer.
Completely packed, they asked of my return to this site? "So I will! All's bound to be right, right here!!
Literally be alright when ME and The Gang's all here at "The Still!" To resound our jolly folly again next year!

Kevin Randall

"Trite Clichés Tripe"

1) I suppose all the professional literary giants will continue to tear apart my prose and rightfully critique my profuse use of such trite vocabulary, just as they do in my prose-reading circle sessions; 2) However, that does not deter my continual march to write using all the right meaningful descriptive (trite included) words I can, just like a golfer will try to use ALL the clubs in their bag in their respective golf rounds; 3) If you really think about it, aren't just about all of the well-known words/ phrases used up by now? How can I help it if our great literary forefathers already spent the best words and phrases? The secret is using the power of any words to produce an original ending to your own story! Right? Think about it – the things that make you go "Hmmmm . . ."

ONCE UPON A TIME . . . you've heard it all before, now hear me again.

If I was you . . . And I'm not . . .

I would try it. Better hold back. Hold on and never let go.

What's it to you? Does anybody really care? Whatever . . .

You are really empowered. How come I can't get out of this rut?

So what 'ya going to do about it?

Try, and try again. If you think you have it rough . . . Why let me tell you!

Don't wanna hear it. C'mon, lend me an ear.

You have an ear for music. You're now singing to the choir.

Couldn't hold a note. On the other hand . . . Silent as a lamb.

Cat got your tongue? Look out! It may scratch your eyes out. Bad luck. Tough luck!

Don't look at me that way. I don't bite.

But I can run. Fast and far. And that's the short of it.

Gimme me a break. Heck no! Do you really think I'm that dumb?

One brick load short. A few cards short of a full deck.

So you got an ace up your sleeve! Now, that I have to see.

Oh! Don't worry about me. Just take care of yourself.

Just Three Words

If you don't, nobody else will.

You just have to keep the will power going.

Going, going, gone. Now what do you have? Nothing. Nuttin' honey.

Don't sweet talk me. Don't talk back. Sassy and frisky, huh!

Won't change. Can't change. Nothing here for me.

Then I'll just take my business down the road.

Somewhere out there. Oh, I'll find my pot o' gold. At the end of the rainbow.

Make it rich, eh! Gonna win the lottery. Then you won't find me. I will make a difference.

Or die trying. Kicked the bucket. Kicked the can. Pushin' up daisies. Flew the coop.

Went to the Netherland. Off to the Promise Land. In a better place.

Oh, who gives a hoot? Staying up late like a night owl! Watch me like a hawk.

Hear me out. It just doesn't make sense.

Somehow this all makes sense. So what's it going to be?

Are you a man or a mouse? Stand up for yourself.

You've made something of yourself. Boy, you've changed.

My, how you've grown! Why, I remember when you were knee high to a grasshopper.

How time has passed? That was so long ago. I forgot.

Where did you end up, anyway? All that, and more. Settle for nothing less.

Give it the ol' college try. You don't win unless you try. Give it all you got.

Ain't got any? Then what good are ya? Oh, you're the best! You rock!

Caught in the middle between a rock and a hard place. No way out.

There's hope over there. I care. Why don't you apply yourself?

Everyone else does. Oh, you think you're better than me? Than them?

I can show them. It's show time! The world's your stage. Break a leg.

Cont.

Heavens to mergatroid! Stage Left. Stay to the right. Stuck in the middle.
Get off the fence. Don't fence me in. I feel all pent up inside.
Let your inner self shine. I took a shining to it. So what's your fave?
Mind you own bee's wax. That's gotta sting. That will leave a mark.
Feel scarred. All squeaky clean. Too clean. Something's fishy.
That smells bad. It is bad. All wrong for you. Let me show you the way.
As the wind blows. Wherever we end up at. Gotta have a plan.
Fail to plan, or plan to fail. Failure is not an option. Heard that before.
You gotta just love it. I can't stand it. So what now?
Now is the time of your life. You're young yet. Boy, how time has flown.
So what time is it? Half past. Tax time. Decisions, decisions.
Can't decide. Take 'em both. The point of no returns.
Been there, done that. Your turn. No U-turn. Can't chicken out now.
Deja vu all over again. Now, that's a cliché!
Have you heard the one about . . . ? I can't hear you! Never mind.
Let's roll. Rock and roll is here to stay. Beat of your own drummer . . .
Step to the plate. Hit a home run. That panned. Loser! From the White
    House to the outhouse.
Leave the door unlocked. Break the doors down. Leave the light on for ya'.
You are always welcome. Stay out. Stay away. Move on. Keep on truckin'.
New horizons. The sun won't set on me. No moss will grow. Before the
    dust settles.
Oh! Where art thee? Over here. Over yonder. Look again.
I can't find it. Why you couldn't find a . . .
Needle in the haystack. The "ayes" have it. An eye for that.
What do you see? Imagining things again? I am NOT making this up. For
    real!
Make believe. Fairy tale. Okay, Alice in Wonderland! Once upon a time . . .

Just Three Words

One by one. Line by line. Many have written these words before.
Proud! Am I to now take my place in history, rewriting scripts, like so?
It's not that I invented any new prose, or really added anymore.
Plain, it's how the words are paired, to make their meaning clearly for us to know.

One by one. Line by line. Hail! To the pioneers who were the first to state their lot.
No ear had heard. No eye had seen. How, new senses came alive, to ever be found.
Don't judge me by what I had penned. It's the same as they had, what's left is what I got.
Marvel at the historical ones who first created such a stir of emotions, to have us thirst for their forever sound.

One by one. Line by line. Now I pass on this wordsmith dare.
To re-use your dictionary, your Pictionary, and be an added visionary to write.
Poems, Prose, Novels, or whatever story forms takes place that you care.
In the end, count yourself among those who won't end the word legacy, but continue the fight.

One by one. Line by line. It's how the words touch your mind, your heart, your soul.
How thankful to our forefathers, who didn't use up all the meanings and how their words be spread.
The testing trek stays alive through us, all the writers who tell their story, to be whole.
Now is the time of <u>your</u> challenge to make your script come alive! Aha!
May <u>never</u> trite cliché tripe remain dead.

Kevin Randall

"... *one small blurb* ..."

1) Thinking back, if you had to personally log each and every day of your life, how would it read? 2) I chose the significance of the eve of attending college, since it was my mom's lifetime dream to have all of her children go to college; 3) Here is an internal look at the beginning of my huge life legacy milestone, since my dorm census was larger than my whole hometown, and the ominous anxiousness of what could this "big campus world" bring? How heartening, and bearable, that softened the worries, was forever found in the enriching lifetime bonding alma mater friendships! Such True Palies!

"one small blurb"

An Editor's Note: One small page of Bio-History . . .
(Page One. Proofed/ Spaced.)
    "... just the right material."
"...Newsworthy. Human Interest. Timely & Current."
"...Precise. Valuable. PRINT!"
College: First Day Eve.
We need the other guy there.
To meet & greet.
To follow his instruction. His direction.
To lead him through doubt. His. Hers. Ours.
To hold a hand in time of need. To lend an ear.
To heed advice.
To brighten our day.
To give him, what we share.
To be there. To care.
To learn, live, hope, dream. To love . . . Together.
Keep the Faith. Pass It on. Keep Smilin'.
We made it this far; thus, now carry on . . .
(Thank you, Lord, for putting such Faith in us.)
To further the Brotherhood of Man.

PRAISE! JOY! THANKS!	AMEN! HALLELUJAH!
Now, onto Day One . . .	Give it the ol' college try!

Kevin Randall

"What Neighbors Say"

1) Hailing from the backwoods country, it's common to see some newer housing next to some older-styled homesteads; 2) "Local" passersby would always know if something might be out of place, like a shiny new car in the driveway; 3) Thus, the neighbor gossip would start . . .

"What Neighbors Say"

I live on the '40 out back.'
Just in a small rundown shack.
You drive that shiny town Cadillac.
"Don't park it here!" is all I'll e'er ask.
    Why, what would the neighbors say?
    Thinking I lost my 'back-country way.'
    Saying it's <u>my</u> new car bling, and all?
    So, don't be parking dat thing near my dirt stall!
I spent a lifetime building my reputation up in these hills.
No rent, or need for TV sitting, work chimes, education, nor pills.
Just fun, bent on dogs a' hunting crimes, and a recreation running my stills.
Being just one at 'bean times,' no table bunting, only varmints' infestation fer filling thy food kills.
    Why, what would the neighbors say?
    Thinking, you and that auto with chrome doors to stay?
    Just know you're here for som' moonshine today . . .
    But, it best if you pull 'round back to stop 'n' pay!
Well, the dogs may make a big fuss.
Howl like the wind at you, they must.
It's not only you . . . me 'n' dem just,
Ain't got used to that upper crust car, dat we don't trust!

    Why, what would the neighbors say?
    Thinking these hills, now gone bad-core some way,
    Stinking new caddy with shiny frills to decay.
    Jest don't park that mo-beel near my still, "okay?"
    Why, what would the neighbors say?

Kevin Randall

"Old Brings New"

1) HAPPY NEW YEAR'S! Truly, one of the most universal worldwide events celebrated; 2) With a glance of reflective nostalgia on the "Old" while we hopefully, peacefully, have gleeful anticipation toward the "New"; 3) Isn't it amazing that we can celebrate the same 'two' occasions in the same way, at the same time, in the same place, with the same people?

"Old Brings New"

OLD YEAR,
    ... Can't take it back;
    ... It has lost its track;
    ... So, Paint it Black.

NEW YEAR,
    ... It is what's just ahead;
    ... It's where we're led;
    ... So, Paint it Red.

When we watch the Eve ball drop, it's more than a mere tall "plop".
As the Old Year sings out its history, it now rings in the New Year legacy.
    Live music, kisses abound, and internet smiles.
    Sights and antics, sounds in different styles for miles.
    New Year is now bright Red! Old Year went night Black instead.

Old Year is now left behind, whether it was cruel or was kind. Just a memory left in our mind . . .
New Year hugs and cheer, a new beginning is right here. New time marching on, so near and clear.
Old Year and New, they are both in our same insight view. Old Brings New – just for Me and for You!

OLD YEAR .... Can't take it back; so, Paint it Black.
NEW YEAR... What's just ahead; so, Paint it Red!

Kevin Randall

"Cross-Stitch Prose Potpourri"

1) In one of my prose reading sessions, a peer reader shared this style of prose; 2) Not hearing so well, I didn't make out that the correct term for this literary prose is "acrostic"... I kinda like my term better, don't you? 3) Being fascinated in this "new" style writing challenge, I took it upon myself to share some of my own cross-stitch, word-wise.

D up dredged dirt	**B** oom! The dynamite	**P** oured polluted water into an
I n between interstate in-rows to	**L** oosened the door	**U** tility urn covered by a sieve to
T rench a water trail to	**A** ttached to the bank	**R** emove rust residue and
C hannel it into a chasm below	**S** afe to loudly shred and	**E** liminate E-coli exposure
H illy high ground	**T** ear it open torridly	

Just Three Words

L egal	**S** haped	**P** eeled??!! Pooh! So, poured
O ver	**C** arved	**A** ll colours artistically together to
A dded	**U** nusual	**I** lluminate illusionary images like a
D umped	**L** ooped	**N** eon sign, neatly
E mpty	**P** ewter	**T** oned and trimmed, and then
D riven	**T** wisted	**S** prayed to a sparkling shine!
	U nveiled	
B rig. Gen & Brigade	**R** adiated	**B** ombing and blasting
A rmy assaulted	**E** tched	**A** ttacking Army
T o thrwart the	**D** edicated	**T** anks and
T errorist tactics		**T** roops and
L ead by legions labeled		**L** ethal legions
E vil enemies of the Empire		**E** merging enemy encounters

Part II

Inspire The Heart

(Live Love Laugh)

Kevin Randall

"Springtime Left Behind"

1) Ah! Springtime, the season of new buds refreshed; 2) We march on to weather any storm, externally or internally, even if the weather is still in a lamb-lioness conflicted turmoil; 3) Sometimes, even with this annual renewal forecasting bright springtime thoughts, we sometimes end up living with unseasonable cloudy results . . . bummer, eh?

In springtime, many years ago;
Springtime, I sent a card to show
The spring in my heart and in my mind;
With hopes for our love to grow.
Ah! The dreams of that springtime,
     so long, so long ago . . .

Time has passed when I held your hand;
In springtime, thought I'd understand
Your warm heart so sweet and kind;
I pledged to be your biggest fan.
My! The dreams of that springtime,
     as a young, young man . . .

Just Three Words

In a young springtime, thoughts of you;
But you said you found someone new.
Hopes dashed in cold springtime
As season colours turned true blue.
Oh! The tears of that springtime,
      all without you, without you . . .

Each springtime I try to keep track.
Now in springtime I still think back;
A budding love, lost and can't find,
Who? Where's the best friend I still lack?
Why? When is the next springtime?
Sigh! This springtime is left behind . . . left behind . . .

Kevin Randall

"This Empty Chair"

1) Not just a chair, but sometimes we are placed in a lonely vantage point of an empty day, or a longing heart; 2) Example of "fullness": go fill a clear jar with rocks and declare it 'full,' then add small pebbles to close the gaps . . . "Full, right!?" Not quite yet, so add in sand so you think the jar is now filled up. Lo and behold, pour in water over all the contents, to the brim, then "Viola!" NOW, the jar of life/ time is totally full! Same as life fulfillment! 3) Help someone 'fill in' substance from their loneliness, and you can be the essential fullness at the time of their life's jar of need! Go, Do It Now!

Sitting there . . .
    All in the dark . . . from this empty chair . . .
Waiting for your call, one blank stare,
    Into the night, so lonely.
Just once, if only you might, you would re-call me.
Please, make the call, pull me, from this empty chair . . . from this empty chair . . .

You had given me hope, some time back.
Needed an escort, for your social track.
    We had been lovers back when. But we grew apart.
    Now, I long for you again. Hoped you had a change of heart.
My plea, is for you to free me, from this empty chair, from this empty chair . . .

Cont.

Kevin Randall

Could that one next date, (oh, please phone), be the needed spark?
Would you change our fate? Or, do I wait, all alone . . . still in the dark?
    Now, change "us" to "forever we," from our one-night affair,
    How I long to be together, you and me, from this empty chair . . .
from this empty chair . . .

Am I dreaming? That we can have a love again to share?
I'm still scheming, dear friend, for you to care. Oh, for how long can I bear?
I desire our love to never end, it being so very rare . . .
Will you inspire to take me from this empty chair . . . ?
Or, do I still stay so mired, only to go on, lonely, from this empty chair . . . this empty chair . . .

"Just Gotta Be!"

1) Most folks' mantra, "Work hard, play hard;" 2) There is an appropriate time to let your hair down; 3) So use a fair balance of family, faith, work, and play, and not be a workaholic like someone else I know. Me. "Don't ever let the spirit grow old!"

There's a day that comes your way.
There's a time on your mind.
When you feel set free to play
And you leave work behind.
Don't hesitate, nor wait and see . . . Don't lose today.
Come on, do what you gotta be. Just gotta be!
    Play time could come this way.
    Don't push the fun away.
    Nor, be too bushed to try.
    Be it, you're sad to say:
        You give up, and you sigh,
        There's chores, in and out;
        Well, don't brood or pout.
Don't hesitate, nor wait and see . . . Don't lose today.
Come on, just do what you gotta be. Just gotta be!
    Keep fun in your heart.
    You're not wrong to play that part.
    Keep style in your smile and in your heart.
Come, play awhile with friends and family.
Don't hesitate, nor wait and see . . . Don't lose today.
Come on, do what you gotta be. Just gotta be!

Kevin Randall

"... don't call me ..."

1) Nicknames can be endearing, yet, they can also make one susceptible to bullying, so parents, beware; 2) What we're called or labeled, nor what we do, doesn't always define us; 3) Usually, it may be best to just live with your own given name, and Be Proud!

(Dedicated to all who hated their childhood nickname)

When I was young, it sounded kinda dumb
I sat on Mama's knee, and this is what she said to me.
"You'll always be, 'My Dear Little One!'"
That was too much for me, "Is that all I'll ever be?"
    Why, I didn't want to be that labeled, or worse,
    "Deer 1?" Lost in some forest? Excuse the pun.
    Part of a nursery rhyme fable? Destined to e'er be in verse?
    Related to a feeble deer named "Bambi"?
    Remembered for carrying Lyme's disease?
    I wanted another name given, oh please! "Pleeeaasse!"
Why don't you call me "King"? Proud like a lion, hear me roar.
Or "Ellie," short for a large Elephant? Ne'er forgetting things in store.
Just don't call me "Deer" . . . getting in headlights, I freeze.
Call me anything else, "Mama! Mama! Won't ya' please?"

Just Three Words

    Like one who climbs daring mountains, as in "Billy" goat.
    Or be known as "Trigger," who sports a mane and shiny coat?
    Give me "Tony," stripes like a tiger cat.
    "O'Smokey," like a bear. I'll wager I'd like that!
"Deer?" Don't lump me in with a winter herd found on the roof top.
Fear. The slump of canter heard, bound at all the other kids' toy stop.
Who wants to be forced to pull a heavy sleigh for an ol' fat man?
Or, "Yikes!" Coerced at having my head weighed as a trophy near a ceiling fan?
    "Mama. Call me "Fido," like a doggy. Such a loyal pet.
    Or by "Spot." You know, I ain't even housebroken yet.
    Now, "Tweetie" bird has a nice ring to it.
    How, you and I can sing a grand musical duet!
Let me be "Scout," like an eagle with soaring eyes;
Not some "Lil Deer" who has stinky little flies.
"Deer?" Forced to run from a schmuck's picky hunting tries.
Yes! I'd rather be "Daffy" or "Flappy," like duck wings heading south.
Just not "My Little Deer," calling me, from your mouth.
    Why, when I 'm grown, I could be like "Alley" the cat,
    Prowling outdoors, not always be on your knee to be sat.
    Address me as "Sir," a penguin with my tux and tie;
    Rather be "Porky" pig, in my own sloppy room and messy sty.

        Cont.

How about "Hippo," a Marx Brothers name?
Or "Buff"–a-lo, who roams with other wild game?
Don't call me "Deer!" It sounds too soft.
I like "Clay" the pigeon sittin' on the barn roof loft.
    "Hoot" owl is a fitting night time handle for me.
    Or "Woody," like the bird hammering on the apple tree.
    "Wolf." "Hennie." "Gator" or "Croc"??
    Just not, "Deer 1" for other's to mock.

I guess by now you got the drift what to call me now.
I just hate "Deer" and what they stand for, and how!

Why, then Mama, looked surprised, as I sat on her knee.
"Oh! Okay. Okay. "My Li'l Sweet Pea!"
    Oh! No! A moniker, dreaded with fear.
    Something liked least, other than, "O' Little Deer!"
    Aw shucks, being referred to as a veggie pea sounds kinda queer.
    And I thought I had been called worse?
    My luck! "Sweet Pea" – a true nickname curse!
… Now what I said next was not for the faint-hearted;
Why, I reeled off ten more verses of nicknames, and I was just getting started!

Morale of Story:
You can't always pick your nickname.
Some are nice, some not so tame.
Just when you think the name is bad,
There could be another to be ashamed.
Sooooo, stick with Mama's "My Little Dear," and just be glad.
Or better yet, keep your real name that you already had!

"Plane + Pilot = Insane?!"

1) You might have seen 'dem 'der aerial daredevils, too, yunno, the crop dusters, and their flyin' circus antics! 2) Incredibly, I witnessed a plane swooping between a construx truck dumping dirt, and the high electrical wires along roadside. "Whew!" He made it . . . a pure miracle of craziness dare; 3) Crazy "crop" pilots don't get insurance, do they, for the stunts they perform? And heck, their plane's a mess, if they still fly, if you can call it that!

The sputtering plane craft wrongly flew thru the sky.
Muttering engine draft, heard long before viewed by eye.
Pilot, so daft, crazily veered that steel bird; "Oh, my!"
Just missed the herd of steer under the trees, where they first lie.
Scary, not knowing if he's in full control,
"Where's he going?" wondered aloud by this earthly soul.
Just when you thought he was going into marshland;
Pulled up. Ramped his height . . . "Almost naught!" "Gosh, I don't understand?"

 This flying "Ace" somehow guided under the wire tie.
This tumbling machine just leaned right on his next blunder fly-by.
That heap of metal stalled and careened, so low barreled to the ground.
Could even see his eyes in the pit; I'm appalled, as he smiled?! "He is just not sound!"

Cont.

Then he sprayed mist on the neighbor's maize and corn.
Didn't care who he scared, with his "near-miss." Not even the grazing cows to my scorn.
Crop duster . . . "Insane!" I shuttered. Just doing his aerial thing.
What a jester, left my heart fluttered, by his dusting flyin' 'territorial' machine.
I breathed now the dusty pass of his dratted fumes a smokin'.
"That heap ain't gonna last," I hissed," What's he bloomin' thinkin'?"

Could barely make out the half-listed logo on the plane.
"Acme Bros!" There's two at this??!! They're real twisted, both must be loco. "They're insane!"
Just then a wind gust blew off his head scarf. It landed in the ditch.
This "Lindy" Acme Pilot, and his pile of rust, flew to make me barf, as if his flight plan had no hitch.

I was still amazed. Shocked, I frowned, as that clown performed another loop.
This time crazed, upside down! Then, what fell down by my feet? "A can of chicken soup?!"
He yelled, "No charge!" as he dusted s'more. "Are you kiddin'?!" I replied.
He just flew into the dust cloud once more. "His brains must be fried!"

Forgot to tell ya' of his duct tape on his wing. "Must help him lean?" I guessed.
How could it fly pell-mell with this scrape and ding? "How is that a flying machine? "That's messed!"
Not hearing his flapping wings anymore, I turned away from his flyin' junk and its smoky air lane.
Now, I have seen it all, and heard sounds hard to ignore; these crazy stunts by Pilot. Plane. "Insane?!"

"Mondays Do Happen"

1) Monday's have a bad reputation, that people oft' dread the day, most notably hungover from a weekend activity overload; 2) being a bus driver, you can even see it in the student's wide array of preparedness to catch the bus on time, some eager and ready, others just coming out of the house on time, and then the few we all wait for, even tho' we all know that Monday's (bus time) does still routinely happen, same-o, same-o; 3) no matter what, I'm just glad they are going to school! Thus, be prepared, get ready and remember each day is good, (any day ending in "y"), and some better than other's... 2 CORINTH 4:16 "...do not lose heart, be renewed, day by day..."

So you were running late. Made others wait. Day not ran smooth at all.
Missed a date. You're in debate. Say, you've taken the fall?
Then a twist of fate. Maybe, at least one thing's great, as you recall.
Mondays Do Happen. Ropes don't slacken, time is at a stall.

    Thinking back. Errands did stack, readied for a weekend break.
    Business off track. Found no slack, all give and no take.
    Then you're in the black. Eased the flack, mind-rest was at stake.
    Mondays Do Happen. Boss is back, so tasks you can't fake. Don't forget his Birthday Cake!

Cont.

No work for a two day span. Saturday and Sunday, begin your chore list.
All work and no play, man. Friday was payday, money in your fist.
Friends can't stay. No matter what they're saying, 'determined' is your gist.
Mondays Do Happen. Work cloud is greying, desk hand-cuffed at the wrist.
Committee work persists!

> Work piled on. Work clothes been don, rest not in sight.
> Tools out of pawn. Work 'til dawn, all through the night.
> Co-workers yawn. Act the fawn, barely see the end light.
> Mondays Do Happen. No hours to spare, slaved with all your might.
> Rest would be a delight!

Jobs done complete. Deadlines were to meet, hung on to compete. You sure did a lot.
Won a rare feat. Covered your seat. Victory smile begot.
Associates to meet. Cleaned up so neat. Little rest upon the cot.
Mondays Do Happen. Filled with time trappings, crossed "Ts" and "I"s with a dot. "A report I forgot?!"

> Now, let us switch gears. Drop your fears, head on home.
> Forget the tears. Picture your dears inward, then text or phone.
> Friends and cheers, stop for beers a-tapping. Rest reward, the dog his bone.

Mondays Do Happen. Your joy uncapping; your survival skills now clearly honed.

Rest is for the "5-day a week" meek, without even a brief pause.
No jest, there's no relief, you shout, "Maybe next week?" . . . 'cause,
Mondays Do Happen.

Just Three Words

"Mailbox Mayhem Madness"

1) Ever since I was a young lad, I have always been fascinated by mailboxes, their styles, shapes, etc.; 2) Then early in my working career, I became a rural mail carrier. During each route, I cautiously opened each box, being aware of whatever might await me from inside; 3) No matter the conditions, it does take a "team" to cohesively work together to get the mail delivered as expected. March On! Mail On!

I.   Oh! No!
There are witches in my mailbox!
      What am I to do?
I found them there this morning,
      doing things they shouldn't do!
How these witches got there?
      I haven't got a clue.
But they won't be there much longer,
      'cause I'm sending them onto you!

II.   Oh! No!
Now, the spiders cry they're so lonely.
      What are they to do?
They miss their mailbox friends,
      those witches, and their brew!
How those l'il spider legs now run so busy
      to carry them through;
'Cause, before, they drank that fun potion,
      Wow wee! They really flew!

Cont.

III.   Oh! No!
Sad, my mailbox is so lonely and empty.
       Mad! So, what's the postman now to do?
He confessed to be goin' crazy,
       without the spiders serving up a new brew!
He used to even stop,
       even if "no flag" was up.
Just to drink some from the brew cup,
       all from the witches view!

IV.   Oh! No!
Now my mailman won't stop at all.
       What am I to do?
Geez, I guess, all for the best,
       I'm walking a letter o'er to you.
Asking ye' to mail back that witches nest,
       to me, for "us", from you!
Pleeze! Give me some rest!
       It is "for the better" thing to do.

V.   Oh! No!
Heck, even my mailbox has been mad at me!
       Okay, smart aleck, "What am I to do?
He covered himself with dust and rust
       for the torment I put his "inner" friends all thru.
(You know, those darn witches, the lonely spiders
       and that Madman Mailman, too!)
Dunno, now, it's I who needs that, "Finally!" brew!
       Yunno, I think you would, too!

VI.   Oh! No!
So, please hurry! Mail those witches thru!
      You just gotta do what you gotta do!
I do worry y'all forget to return the gang's fave, too?
      You, know that hotta tangy, witches brew!

VII.   Oh! No!
To my surprise, all from those witches being 'mis-sent';
      Air Mail, we actually did invent!
All from this unlikely crew:
Witches. Spiders. Postman. Mailbox . . . and me, too!

VII.   Oh! Yes!
We are all happy, now that we are re-united.
      Can't believe what sappy riot I had ignited!
The moral of the story: Hang with <u>ALL</u> the gang in glory!
      Never start a coup!
Smile with style. Co-exist, as family do.
      That will ease any rue.
Remember too, thru rain, thru sleet, thru snow, and even thru witches brew;
You gotta do what you gotta do . . .
      The mail must go through!

Kevin Randall

"Every Body Lookin' "

1) Just looking at the poem context, we are natural people watchers; 2) When you do, be prudent, be logical, and be appropriately sensible; 3) So, remember when the tides are changed, and you are on stage! Be good about it.

Every body looking, every one for sure.
Every love is working, to make their love secure.
    Then reality sets in, there's a knockin' at the door.
    Should love "go by" or "be let in?" Would love enter within?
Some say it's a 'game of hearts,' so let chips fall where they may.
Others, look toward the stars, to let love wait for a rainy day.

Gathered no magic cards or horoscopes read; nor, be of dreamt time capsule parts.
Rathered, bestowed safety guards to watch where they lead, in minds, bodies, hearts.
    All for the love of woman and manhood; God made such art!
    Your love, finally, fully, understood: 'til death do us part!'
Your search maybe forever, until it feels 'right.' Turning the corner, a 'find' could even be tonight.
Reached your lover through sight; through rejoiced voices that garner; minds and hearts to make it alright.

In a lifetime journey, in togetherness, happiness can abound;
Even thru the briny, rough sea, thru the weariness of tough ups and downs.
At first, joined as one union, then a possible split; only to harmonize again.
Rehearsed your reunion to become a big hit; opened minds, hearts, and bodies to realize attention.
> Finally, re-meet as one to become a pair; then onward in the same direction, to proceed.
> Ultimately, complete love shared, outward, in the same action, voice, and in (act) deed!

Now, go forth as a love, weathered and strong in the making.
How to do right by your partner, atone and forgive for a wrong . . . 'cause, every body is lookin'!

"Against The Grain"

1) Most times, it is probably 'comfy' being a conformist; 2) You are possibly considered living on the edge, when you do go 'against the grain'; 3) So, use wisdom, experience, to be your own person to stand out from the crowd; thus, Be Good, Be Safe, Be Kool, making a name for yourself in a positive manner.

"Against The Grain"

Did you ever think you're bold enough,
To stand up, and go 'against the grain'?
Although the mighty crowd may call your bluff,
You've landed at the age, 'lest not to refrain.
      Of course, pick and choose the right times;
      To not deter, succumb, or sway.
      What is there to lose, not become a mime,
      But, set your own course, and be on your way.
You need to squeeze the knob of opportunities door,
To aim for new heights abound.
Heed your courageous soul, never to turn around,
and reach for goals you shouldn't just ignore.
      Others are proud that you even tried a feat,
      Some with envy, and some express disdain.
      Deep inside, they wish they hadn't remained in their seat,
      but embraced the dare to stand and go 'against the grain.'
Each day brings you challenges to bear,
Say, "nothing to venture, nothing to gain."
Ever, steadfast on the road many do share,
You pass the test on our own path, 'against the grain.'
      You'll trace back someday, to see what you have done.
      Say "YES!" Be content that you even tried to compete.
      Many twists and turns along the way, not always fun,
      SUCCESS! Your long journey, 'against the grain,' is now complete.

Kevin Randall

"My Friend Jack"

1) I always try to be a dependable servant leader in delivering customer service excellence; 2) In this story, a great short-lived friendship grew from performing simple tasks and errands for a shut-in; 3) which resulted in lasting endearing memories around our bonding, initiated from my fortunate random work assignment. You never know, when a "new friendship" can happen to you.

I was summoned to clean his house, at first.
Entered slowly. He moaned, pointed for water to clear his thirst.
The lights dimmed so lowly down. Cat on his lap, Jack sat with a lonely frown.
All three quiet in that room, I kept on dusting through such gloom, without a sound.

Yes, Jack's sister requested that I was to track the hours I cleaned for him.
Jack and I became buds sequestered; looking back, our memories at a minimum.
Oh, it seems just like yesterday on the phone,
Called to clean a house, ". . . make it a Home."
So, thru polished rooms and hearts, day by day, in a way, we were friends, ne'er alone!

Each time there on site, I quickly wiped the sink, the stove, the table.
Shining bright! To help My Friend Jack, what he was not able.
As I quietly dusted and mopped the floor, we bonded silently in just one week.
The cat's rusted squeak implored; the only noise that blended with Jack trying to speak.

My Friend Jack breathed so slooow, his darkened room a tomb-set; "Time to goooo?" he rued. "No," I harkened, "my chore work ain't done yet."
He gazed and eyed one more time around. Even cried to speak again through his frown.
He tried to smile at this time, with no sound, tho' his spirits were so down.
My thought . . . "we're not far behind" . . . so, same how goes my cleaning tasks be wound . . .

I softly took his twisted hand, so cold, to help him clean his bedside slate. To allow this next life chapter to unfold. I winced to know his final tide of fate.
"Meow," the shiny cat still in his lap;
When, Jack took his last sigh before his "forever" nap.
Then, my heart beat for two. I whispered, "My Friend Jack, I'll miss you."

Funny, now looking back, on when we met. How we talked, even in mime, so little.
Keeping hours tracked, cleaning times were set. Yet, speech balked, our 'we' time, so brittle.
But even in silence, 'dust to dust,' we sulked, to let life tarry on to settle.

Sunny, on this today; mentally, I return to his dark room.
A happy memory, I ever carry, cleaning through such gloom.
In a way, I really yearn for each day to go back.
Smiling, I'm still so teary, 'bout weaning from "My Dear Friend, Jack!"

"Best Kept Secret"

1) Life lessons, are found in the most inexplicable times. That is why tough situations are considered "as opportunities . . . of growth;" 2) Always be prepared, that as a "listening" parent, that your reaction in handling an "issue," brands you as a role model, good or bad; so act wisely, and with empathy; 3) Ps 90:12~ "Teach us to number our days aright, that we gain a heart of wisdom."

She bent over him in a hug,
    to whisper within only his ear-shout.
The smile from her, his timid shrug,
    such 'keeper love' that you hear about.
He was a "first-time" 4K student
    just boarding the school bus in the morning.
"He was to remain good 'n' prudent,"
    I guessed, of her private fair warning.
A scene of non-regret,
    a memory that they won't forget,
"Serenity." One of Mom and son's Best Kept Secret!

Another growing up story,
    coming home in tears,
        she climbed the weary stairs
To tell of her big worry.
    Having to brave it alone, with fears,
        chimed, "Who really cares?"
Full well, knowingly Mother,
    sensing the young lady
        needed a face to face,
Approached slowly, not to smother,
    wincing, to hear Fawn lost "her steady;"
        such a sad case.
How could she return tomorrow?
    To work with the bad guy,
        who created a "mad" lie?
How to go on feeling burned up in sorrow,
    ". . . that jerk should fry!"
        elevated in her cry.

Tissues, and a pillow case all wet,
    a memory that they won't forget,
"Teen issues." One of Mom and daughter's Best Kept Secret!

Dad's away on a business trip.
    Sonny taking a small mall loop
        in the family sedan.
Glad that he got his license slip.
    Funny, making a call, then "whoops!"
        He ran into a smelly can.
Hopped out to get a view.
    "Oh! No!" The front bumper dent;
        yet, only spilled out the can content.
Mopped up, sweaty, "P-U!"
    Ego, brunt of this thumper accident;
        fret to return home, to lament.
Told Mother of his misadventure;
    parked car in the shed,
        to hide his tall shame.
Bold Mom eyed this indenture,
    "Marked and scarred, nothing bled;"
        a ride of just small blame.
"Pay you back, to your wishes," Sonny exclaimed.
    Mom: "We subscribe to insurance, but I will keep track."
"Spray 'n' stack the dishes," many chores to be named.
    "No prom drive to the dance! The bill, for that car crack."
The repair was made
    before Dad returned.
        Mom & Sonny kept quiet 'bout his accident.
Both aware of the bumper new shade.
    "Chore lessons" Sonny had learned.
        He soon worked off his debt.
Sweaty palms, exercise of humility, a memory they won't forget.
"Reality calm." One of Mom and Sonny's Best Kept Secret!

Sissy wanted 'a few cookies for school;'
    "To bake for sell at a band date,"
        a yearly "Symphony Meal & Show."

Cont.

Mommy daunted, knew this rookie needed a tool,
    to make morsels "chewy great!"
        Added in deary Granny's family recipe dough.
While the two worked together
    in the kitchen so hot,
        the batch came out just right!
Smiled, the "chew" time couldn't have been better;
    a recipe of love they got!
        To catch the same again? "Outta sight!"
Actually blended, work & fun, stirred in a story of Granny's Pride, like she was at their side!
    Lived a memory they won't forget.
Recipe faring intended, and occurred!
    "Proud Sharing Tradition."
        One of Mom and Sissy's Best Kept Secret!

A rejoiced child selection!
    devised renewed parent adoption,
        a new family just the same.
A choice of determination,
    revised transparent adaption,
        really took on a new name.
Added another to feed in the clan.
    Weighed and Nurtured,
        duly refreshed, when re-trained in old "baby" habits.
Gladdened to heed what they can.
    Portrayed and Matured,
        truly meshed, then re-gained their sanity wits.
Hooked on apparent co-existence,
    taught older sibling
        to not mention, "baby on loan,"…
Took on a different sustenance,
    sought to cover-up any inkling,
        "just say, one of our own!"
What will the Neighbors say?
    "How in Peoria will it play?"
        The all above, they to play their parts.
With this new "labor for baby,"
    show their euphoria is here to stay.
        Same love display in their hearts.

A renewed "Welcome Home" past!
    Engrained, "never alone;" "OK" bargained,
        to shove a lot into life's re-starts.
A Family with a new one in cast,
    never a "second" of regret,
        cuddling memories they won't forget.
"A new History Tree, and silence bridging the past."
    One of Mom and Dad's Best Kept Secret!

A call home,
    late in the eve,
        woke a slumbering household.
All alone,
    hate and grieve,
        spoke of numbering days to unfold.
The big "C" was the news
    about a parental one
        who had cared for her in yesteryears.
Sick in misery, Ma's to lose
    out, apparently so stunned,
        both shared a mirror of tears.
Together, decided
    to soldier on thru the pain,
        the best they could.
Prayers recited,
    mold her last days, to gain
        the rest they should.
Stronger in love,
    planned time alone
        in solitude.
Pushed, came to shove,
    expanded their mind tone
        with new attitude.
Voiced song of Bible verse,
    to ask for reverse;
        yet, have no life regret…
Poised, in love immersed,
    a memory not to forget,
"Life Rejoiced!" One of Both Moms' Best Kept Secret!

Kevin Randall

"Two Tables Over"

1) I have dined many times solo, and have on occasion, witnessed certain eateries that specifically offer a table for "single folk" to join others at a larger table, to enhance everyone's dining experience; 2) So, step up to the plate, and ask another "single diner" to join you, if appropriate, 3) and let the visitors be victorious in sharing their just desserts of togetherness!

Waved for my Server,
"Come closer. Hear my offer."
"Had noticed the Young Lady."
"Another cup of tea, 'On me!' "
From the guy two tables over.

Only wanted a simple answer.
Oh! Gee! Not to be a bother!
Only that the Lady, be happy for the tea;
And, smile back at me.
Yes, to see me, two tables over.

Then the Waiter made the offer,
From my coffer,
From my simple plea.
Then I saw the Lady,
She seemed to waiver, Oh, Dear me!

Cont.

Kevin Randall

Waved for my Server,
"Come closer. Hear my offer."
"Had noticed the Young Lady."
"Another cup of tea, 'On me!' "
From the guy two tables over.

Only wanted a simple answer.
Oh! Gee! Not to be a bother!
Only that the Lady, be happy for the tea;
And, smile back at me.
Yes, to see me, two tables over.

Then the Waiter made the offer,
From my coffer,
From my simple plea.
Then I saw the Lady,
She seemed to waiver, Oh, Dear me!

Cont.

Just Three Words

Drat! Hoping she's not a hater
At my gesture through the Waiter?
Be mature. She must be the Lady, I figured her to be.
Debating, "Just smile back at me,"
Waiting, I was two tables over.

Just then her face she did cover.
Mouthing some words to the Waiter.
I couldn't clearly see.
Yearning out, cried, what could the answer be?
Leaning in, tried to keep my cool, barely, two tables over.

I felt such a downer, my brow, a big frowner.
How would I ever recover?
Until I heard the Young Lady
Smiling so nicely at me,
Hearing her now closer, "Move Over!"

I was now smiling from each lip corner!
Wow! I will have to tip my Server!
For that Young Lady
Was now sitting next to me!
Smiling together, no longer two tables over!

Kevin Randall

"Gravel Hill Cabin"

1) My maternal grandparents lived on Gravel Hill Farm, and we grandkids always felt a special trip was in store whenever we got to go visit; 2) I imagined Grandpa back in his younger days, sharing a proud moment of thanksgiving in his new life with Grandma, looking out from an imaginary porch, upon the blessed land they farmed; 3) with grit and grace, together they could smile about a good day's work being done and the good life they both endured as good stewards of God's country! Read EPH 5:19-20

"Gravel Hill Cabin"

I see my log cabin over by Gravel Hill.
I sit there thinking "done a good days work," all until . . .
    Morning dawn finds me out there again.
    Feeding the stock, working the land.
And, breathing in all this fresh air from Gravel Hill's till.

But, for now, the cabin porches are my haven;
Just rest, from the farming toils and thy slaven'.
    My 'partner,' the Good Lord, I am fore'ver thankin.'
    One who blesses us with any fruitful soil, we're ever cravin'.
And, breathing in all the fresh air as the Gravel Hill maven

I am not alone in a Farmer's Thanksgiving Prayer.
Many others know of the riches planted "out there."
    The crops they had reaped to share.
    The time invested in animal care.
And, living with a Good Woman, breathing in all this fresh Gravel Hill air.

The woman of Gravel Hill makes it all worthwhile.
She works hard, too; yet, keeps her ways so mild.
    We break bread together in Family-style.
    She eases the pains; and, helps on paperwork to file.
And, we're all breathing in the Gravel Hill fresh air, always with a smile!

Kevin Randall

"Share A Moment"

1) Always had some 'high-anxiety' when it came to asking a lady out for a date; 2) Yet, I kept faith in myself, that I could muster up just the right courage to approach her. In this story instance, I took a brave chance on asking a "very busy" lady out for some shared time of fun; 3) To my surprise, she answered affirmatively, immediately; however, what is still pending is that I desire for her to keep her end of the bargain and pick the right timing that we can share a moment . . .

So what did I mean when I said, "Let's go for a bite?"
I guess I didn't fully explain that this meant, this week, maybe, even tonight?
You had said "YES!" without a doubt.
Now, I still await your call. Somehow, I still feel left out.
All I desire is for us to Share a Moment of fun delight.

Together real soon. Not lose sight of 'our time.'
C'mon, that's not a crime.
However, my memories would be so sublime.
I will step aside if you want me to not relent.
All I desire is for us to Share a Moment well spent.

I really don't wish to wait. The better, uh, the best time, I think, is real soon.

Hey, what do you think of our date? "How 'bout a sodie drink over some noon?"

Guess I'll have to come back to this "awaiting dating" later. You said your schedule's so full.

Yes, there's just gotta be a time when you'll wanna catch your breath, finally get a lull.

All I desire is for us to Share a Moment, either under sun or moon.

You were in such a rush. I didn't get your number.

You took mine to 'feel safer?' Maybe I was dumber?

Why didn't I press you for an exact time and date?

I was trying to be nice, I guess. Forsake plans for the present, yet, not make you late.

I confess my sure true desire, for us to Share a Moment. Otherwise, what a bummer!

Kevin Randall

"Perils Of Paradox"

1) A simple dictionary example of a paradox, is "more haste, less speed;" 2) So I took it to a very complicated state, imagining what one 'long ago' lover might be thinking of on what to say, to get "orchids out of onions" from a long overdue anticipated upcoming re-union; 3) One mate counts to "10" things to say, when maybe what he really needs to concentrate on is what she may say. Especially, since in this delicate case, a lot is riding on their civil coexistence communication, when custody/visitation of their child is involved. Negotiation, prayer, and empathy skills are needed at a premium.

He made in his voice a vow to be heard.
Not trade his choice, or give up on his word.
His heart still beats with deep life inside.
Not part with defeat, nor, let his feelings subside.
      Been many years, yet his mind goes back . . .
      Not for the tears, but for just losing track . . .
      He wonders, how will she look at his face today?
      He ponders, until, he thinks of what she will say?

Just Three Words

He counts to Ten ideas of what she'll state then:
1. You're still a lone dream man that went astray
2. Two hearts, too heavy to weigh
3. Simple, care to remain 'free'
4. Before, there was a 'you and me'
5. High-Five, a glad hooray
6. A devil hex, a mad boo-ray
7. Roll of dice, relive some paradise
8. "Too late" vs. "That's great" in her eyes
9. Draw the line, boundaries for his time
10. He pens her still, "Will she take him back again . . ?

Numbered ways for patience; for this hour reunion.
Poetic pause, the essence of a "flower orchid or sour onion?"
What will her answer be? Now, it's he, that is waiting for she.
Will it reoccur? He prays for a repeat of good history, for sure.
Does she know that he wants his daughter back? Let him count the ways where's he's at.
Does she ever waiver, and think there were events that made him disappear?
Today, so eager, he hopes to try to explain when she is near.
He was the bad guy, who left in despair. Told to live elsewhere, she didn't care.
He left hurt and sadness in his wake. Today, he's changed, to give more than take.
When she's near, he must atone for sins and fear, to amend, for time being apart.
Again, his repeat vow is to repair now, to mend, their both broken heart.

Kevin Randall

"Bus Bingo Boogie"

1) What else do you expect from a school bus driver? How come we don't have our own polka song?! 2) So you think this is easy, try it sometime, with a loaded bus, and an occasional storm a-brewing; 3) Little bit of fun to play with all the bus numbers that are messaged each day, and "quietly," too? School Bussin' – one of the best jobs in America! So sing it with me, won't ya'? "Bus Bingo Boogie!"

All the buses entered the school drive.
Being called out, some with a 9, a few with a 5.
The busses all come together to make a puzzle fit.
No matter the weather, the students board on to hustle and sit.
Safety First! Respect and Pride!
How they seem to not forget the right numbers of their ride.
Maybe, 'cause they're painted on their front, back, and side.

Most have 1 in their sequence, followed by a zero some call "Oh."
"B" for bus, and hence, they play the "Bus Bingo Boogie!"

Just Three Words

Each bus calls in for a radio check. Heaven's forbid if there's a bus alarm that might go to heck!

Some trouble shootin' ideas exchanged, and before you know it, another bus has been arranged.

Whole new number set then called into play. Save the broken bus back for a-fixin' to run on another day.

2-4-6 then 8. Any numbers ending in 2-0; well, we call it "20."

More recited numbers across the air wave, 9-7-5-3, and we're all playing "Bus Bingo Boogie!"

Run those routes, kids quiet, Shhhh! Never pout or shout!

Roulette numbers over and over are said. Busses running day or night, over the roads they have sped.

8-4-1-4, call out "56" or "99" and 3-3-5 once more.

We got student for a 7-3-1, we need a driver for this afternoon's day fun?

Well, call up 4-6-7; that bus just might be heading for the pick-up next to the 7-11?

2-4-6 and 8. Any numbers ending in 2-0; well, we call it "20."

More recited numbers across the air wave, 9-7-5-3; and, we're playing "Bus Bingo Boogie!"

Then 1-0-5-3, it has some message about the detour history.

Before you know it, all the busses are on time to the minute.

Call in to "BASE," asking for student phone info, then 26-43 has run into construction misery.

Don't fret, just have to wait a moment, then replay more numbers for "Bus Bingo Boogie!"

2-4-6 and 8. Any numbers ending in 2-0; well, we call "20."

More recited numbers across the air wave, 9-7-5-3; and, we're all playing "Bus Bingo Boogie!"

Cont.

This chatter goes on all day. Some like to hear the radio numbers, others wish it wouldn't play!

No matter the day ending in "Y," there's a bus out there in reply, stating their number "All Clear."

Why, sooner or later, all the numbers seem like a cheer! They become sweet music to hear.

That's if you're into the number game, if not what a shame! Since we all wait for our numbers patiently, 2-4-6 then 8. Any ending in 2-0; well, we call it "20."

More recited numbers across the air wave, 9-7-5-3; and, we're all playing "Bus Bingo Boogie!"

Sing it with me as we go round and round the round-about, drivers looking and students hanging out,

As we play "Bus Bingo Boogie!" 2-4-6 and 8. Any numbers ending in 2-0; well, we call "20!"

More recited numbers across the air wave, 9-7-5-3; and, we're all playing "Bus Bingo Boogie!"

Let's all play the "Bus Bing Boogie!" Sing it with me, "Bus Bingo Boogie!" "Bus Bingo Boogie!"

"Just In Time"

1) Timing is so important in life; 2) We are all growing in time AND going on time; 3) Thus, age gracefully, and keep the faith and hope that love will enter at any time.

Woke up in the morn
Ever since we were born
Want time to stand still
Love will come in time,
Just in Time.

looking for love today.
we seek it that way.
to enjoy more of love's thrill.
someway, any day, it will.

Normally, starting out trying to find
Usually, we're the one left behind
Really, slow on what to say,

a friend just for the fun.
always being on the run.
one way love doesn't stick
around to stay.

Truly, love will come in time
Just in Time.

someway, anyway, it will.

"In Your Circle"

1) The all-powerful cliques that are built, in our schools, and in our workplace, can be quite decisive to productivity and blinding us, and hindering us to realizing more added real friendships; 2) So, let's put my circle with your circle and "viola!" We may have something here that is agreeable to widen our horizons of friends and life! 3) Yes, Strength is still in the Quality of Friendships, not how many! So why exclude someone the possibility of being a valued friend? Don't limit the possibility of new friendships by never looking beyond your own clique.

IN YOUR CIRCLE you
will find many Friends so fine. I feel I
would know this of the "Who?" and "Where?"
that they are, because of the ones similar found
in the same Circle as mine. In your Circle is so special,
made from loyal particles, because "it's yours!" formed from
your own interiorical cliques. Theoretical, not radical, then see
if you feel logical and feasible about our own respective Circle,
being so spherical, when we match and mix? I say that we would be
more symmetrical in one Circle, joining my Circle in your Circle. Being
admirable, my Circle could be In Your Circle, statistically speaking,
raising vertical the number of Friends in multiples, becoming one large
"our" Circle . . . Not trying to be an oracle, I foresee one large spectacle
when our Friends do meet reasonable as one Circle. Nothing drastical,
not dramatical, nor theatrical, just harmonically, spectacular! So, let's
put out our tentacles, to see if the each Circle can act responsible,
chime in like a hymnal canticle and grow my circle into your circle
to become Our Circle, identical! Wouldn't that be fun! Thus,
through this miracle, we become supernatural in Circle of
Friends! My Circle is looking forward to with great
anticipational, stoical patience, to join in your
Circle to be that one magical "our" Circle!
Fantastical!

Kevin Randall

"She's So Amazing"

1) Being a nostalgic person and a romantic wannabe, I have a mental charismatic image of a "perfect" woman; 2) a real "keeper," with such lovable, admirable traits; 3) My only hope is that I can live up to her best "imaginary great guy" characteristics that she has on her list.

She's so amazing!
Her warmth and affection,
Is what I feel;   as I softly nuzzle by her ear.
Her sweet aroma,
Is what I really sense;   as she draws so close, so near.
Her soft words,
Stir my very soul,   as that's what I like to hear.
Her lips so fine,
Kisses real divine;   as a taste of affection to endear.
Her pure loving heart,
Breathes a fire inside;   as it paints a pretty picture so clear.
Her deeply focused eyes,
Casts a profound spell;   as it eases my every fear.
Put her all together,
She is of regal class;   as a lovely, sensual dear.
She's so amazing!
She stirs my every sense;   as such an amazing dear!
She's so amazing!

"I'm So Free"

1) We all can have some very intense family life, being involved in so many diverse activities; 2) We need to slow down, heed rest, when it is the right time, to balance life with some earned R&R time; 3) Oscar Wilde quote: "Life is too important to be taken seriously." Enjoy your times together, time flies by . . .

YIPPEE! I'm so free!

Meal is done.
Mate is gone.

Kid's off to school.
Home alone . . . How Cool!

Quiet is the day.
Hobby. Work.
Go for a walk.
Write the book.
Drive to the shore.
Lure. Swing. Ball.
Yippee! I'm so free!

Now, what I want to do!
Go play!
Or, a neighborhood talk.
Prep a new look.
Sleep in some more.
Pray. Read. Mall.
Yippe! I'm so free!

Dream. Pray.
Paint. Cook.

Love anew.
Sing. Canoe.

The list goes endlessly.
Yippee! I'm so free!

Now, is the time "for me."
Yippe! I'm so free!

Kevin Randall

"Accept Loves Memory"

1) Realizing that sometimes love never leaves us, it is 'just sleeping;" 2) just like in this tale of sweet love that may come back someday; 3) "You can give without loving, but you can never love without giving." ~ Anon

"... We will not be remembered by our words, but by our kind deeds."
"Life is not measured by the breaths we take; rather, by the moments that take our breaths away."

Just when I take your call,
    and I think you are on your way,
That's just the time I recall,
    you blinked again, and you pushed me away.

Something else going on, I guess?
    "You're busy. Maybe another day? Life's a mess."
Then, when I think we are finally through,
    you came over and asked me to stay with you.

It's so darn hard to wonder we had any love at all.
> Busted hearts, but we still stood tall.
"How grandeur our life was as a pair!"
> Trusted loving memories that we did share!

To renew again, and recreate our love to come alive,
> we must 'let go' to freely grow.
It's more than passing thoughts, 9 to 5,
> just to let our hearts glow. That we both used to know.

Likened to a ripened seed that we had sown,
> we accepted each other's role.
We faced our mantra creed, toe to toe,
> we expected one's love to enter the other's soul.

Remembering the good with the bad,
> we must review our relationship history.
Through the tears and smiles of glad,
> we trust anew, for our hearts to accept loves memory.

Kevin Randall

Part III

Enrich The Soul

(Faith Fortitude Forever)

Kevin Randall

"Fire Flare Flame"

1) Deep meditation/contemplation at a retreat to regain "Good Hope/ New Hope;" 2) Always attracted by the simple symbolic faith signs of fire and water, and in this case, the Flame was the centering attention that I needed to reflect upon for His helping hand to lift my spirits up; 3) I yearn that when tested on "faith" and "hope" and "grace" that I can "F.R.O.G." (Forever Rely On God) and lean on His ever-guiding Words of Light. *"The Lord is radiant, gives us light to show our way." ~ Kahil Gibran*

A semicircle of folk on a chilly Friday night,
Everyone tired from the week, anxiously with fright.
What to expect? No time to think. "Hi" to a new friend.
Then, pull up a chair, recite names . . . the time doesn't end . . .
    I focus on the Flame – the Light of God – so close to me.
    I feel the heat, no matter where I sit to choose to see.
    People bleed their hearts that were spurning, hurting, broken.
    He warms the heart with this burning, yearning token.
Flame! Burn so bright, Flare return through this blight.
In Fire, my fingers do singe; yet, in warmth my heart heals a tinge.
I clear my throat, concentrate my aim, to hear my heart beat.
Near the Fire, Flare, Flame, I swear it never felt so sweet!
    Lots of feelings surface in facing the Flame – our Real Life Maker.
    Please, Fire, burn so bright! You truly are my heart caretaker.
    This day's Flare brings me closer to Thee.
    Hurry Flame, burn this fog off of me!

Cont.

Flame, Flares so high, the Fire light so straight and tall.
I can now touch you, and your sparking sprawl.
This lit candle leads me through a new door ajar.
You get to lead me, no matter how near or afar.
> Big Flare shared with me from God above.
> Oh! Flame, you are now my friend, my love.
> Fire, burn the 'garbage,' I put out on the street.
> Light my way, and for all that I do meet.

Tonight, we share this time with new friends.
How right! Fire, Flare, Flame has become our means to the ends.
How lucky we are to see this life anew.
Beautiful Flame! Really, we couldn't have done this without you.
> Some slip away, to be on their own.
> I stay close to the Flame, and how it's shown.
> Tight togetherness, the Flare shows His care.
> Such happiness, this Flame does glow to share.

Wow! Your Flare aura is felt with such might.
Dear Lord, You are so close through Your Flame of Light!
Physically, the candle light actions looks so small.
Mentally, we picture your mighty reflections upon the wall.
Spiritually, the Fire, Flare, Flame, without slight detections, ever burning for us all!

"His True Magic"

1) "Do the best . . ." ~ Helen Keller 2) Keep Hope in today, it is the Present! 3) "By Hope, we are kept young at heart, for it teaches us to trust in God, to work with all our energies, but to leave the future to Him." ~ Gerald Yawn

Woke up this morning, with nothing to matter.

'Long ago' memories stirring, before they began to shatter.

Slowly, wiping the devil's dust from my sleepy eyes.

Growingly promised anew, by the 'vow' rust, that I now could recognize
      the new person in me; to give my heart all that I should flatter.

I pledged to myself, "Today!" is what I would surely enjoy.

Every moment, every way. Only then could I set forth my energy ploy.

I began to transform myself into something others should see.

'Cause, I decided to become Someone! One, who accepted the Good Lord in me.

Thus, I felt such a difference, hence, His True Magic began to employ.

Cont.

Kevin Randall

I can feel a new beginning when holding onto His Powers.
I know right away His True Magic works through all our living hours.
How could I have sight, yet not had seen such beauty within?
A Good Life living, yet, just 'NOW!' have energy to re-begin!
Clearer meaning given to let His True Magic enter within ours.

Not to heed a sleight of hand, secret dust, nor wand or stick,
All I needed was a <u>mirror case</u>, a <u>prayer card</u>, and <u>His True Magic</u>!
First, I had to reflect on myself, face to face; for, that's whose life I share.
Then, I spoke with the Lord to repent, ask forgiveness, guidance, and for His care.
Oh! Wow! What an answer – His True Magic! Now, that's the Spirit! He's so terrific!
Yes! It's up to you, too, if you chose, to use this small trick.
Remember, the Good Life, is filled with all His True Magic!

"Gift Of Change"

1) We all own the 'gift of change;' 2) So step up, step out, exercise that right, and share – spread your talents of faith and hope and love to someone in need; 3) That what you receive, give as a gift. Your reward is in Heaven!

A gentle breeze brought the calm of day,
      a special time indeed.
A small sign appeared along our way,
      a miracle born from a tiny seed.
A haze kept the sun far away,
      instead, brought a colorful shade of light.
The magic of the moment came to stay
      tho' some characters played out of sight.

Slightly, endlessly, we watched for Nature's sign.
Eventually, finally, we heard distant sounds in time.
We waited so still, so as not to stir;
Yet, awakened life's new thrill, sprung like a growing caterpillar.

Cont.

Oh! The beauty of life mystery,
        how Our Master's love unfolds His hand!
Grow yields aplenty, like a butterfly so free,
        to flitter above this earthly land.
This evolution plants such a thought
        of how life exists about
This transition is a symbol wrought
        in how Nature develops its own clout.
The visions we use, limited, cannot always see things are honed.
The freedom from within, spirited, can bring forth and be our own.

THE GIFT OF CHANGE –
The talents are many, we all seem to possess.
The cares we lend and carry, to help others through cold and emptiness.
The thought of a dear friend's worry and tarry, we can calm with tenderness.
In shared life, to marry, and to help mold change, no matter the address.

THE GIFT OF CHANGE –
We've been told to Preserve,
        to not give up on Trust.
Compassion, a fine quality in reserve,
        to develop it a must.
Possess Diligence,
        to make our remorse, blight journey better.
Not be remiss on Conviction,
        to stay the course, right to God's letter.

Mix in a little bit of Creativity and Resilience,
> to make the Gift Of Change be labeled: YOU!

'Lest not nix, nor forget, our Mentor's hand of Vigilance,
> to stir this life-long stew.

Keep yourself Accountable,
> to stay in full command,

Add in Forbearance,
> to help us take a stand.

Discernment,
> to keep alert and aware.

And, you will grow a lot inside,
> to help life's heart care.

Now, top off your Gift of Change, to accept God, and be aware, He is our Grace-filled Steward to share.

THE GIFT OF CHANGE –

Let's take this lesson a step further,
> to be an open invite for others to see.

Fully inspect all that surrounds us, hither;
> to specially be in the lives of you and me.

My talent is to word this just right,
> to help us better understand,

To bring forth delight, day and night,
> to catch the beauty in our own hand.

To share such a sight, to bring it all alive,
> to be that person, to believe in God's plan.

Cont.

Kevin Randall

A goal not easy to reach,
      to not be named so strange.
To mold, empower, not preach,
      But to live the Gift of Change.

What do you have to lend and offer,
      to come forth, and make life anew?
So many are sharing their talent coffer,
      to launch their ship, without you?
Step up and give and steer,
      to help others in hardship get through.
Some close, others not so near,
      to give yourself to them as your gift.
Tho' it may sound so canned, so managed,
      to share inner beauty as your Gift of Change uplift.
The trip will be long; the journey somewhat strange.
      To feel the magic, go unwrap your Gift of Change.

"All Is Silent"

1) My favorite poetry piece! Growing up in rural farmland America, what better miracle to witness than the growth from seeds! 2) This prose composition came so quickly, as did many others surrounding the theme of Mother Nature, and how God has a never-resting hand in our lives; 3) Miracles do happen, even when we are not fully aware of them, so please cherish one and all, don't take them for granted.

The flower seed hits the ground
Somehow burrows without any sounds.
Planting His seed all around,
Gods' work in silence just abounds.
All before the sun goes down.
All is silent. "All is right," He astounds!

Rain falls quietly from His skies;
Growth happens when we don't realize.
Miracles wrought before our very eyes.
He shows His love through this disguise.
A rose blooms from effort He applies.
All is silent. "All is right," He cries!

He still works through the night.
Dewing growth as we sleep tight;
Giving us rest, while He uses might.
Raising a flower in sun and starlight;
Creating a bud as bees take flight.
All is silent. "All is Right." He is right!

"Grand! Grand! Grand!"

1) "GRAND!" is the best definition I thought of for a Holy Marriage celebration; 2) and the solemn oath that two share living His Word, so I wrote this for a dear friend's wedding; 3) Through God's blessings, this couple have had such grand life's joy to share happily ever after! *Ps 37:4 ~ "Delight in the Lord, He will give you the desires of your heart and soul."*

O'Lord, You are such wonder of fame.
We heard Your calling from above.
Shine on! Mighty is Your name!
O'Lord, we are falling, ever in love.
Shine on! How grand is Your flame!
You are such a wonder. You made this day.
    Through You, we made grand plans for us to say:
    "I love you!" Today, to a special friend.
All this came through You, and Your love, without end.
O'Lord, You are such a wonder. Shine on! How grand are You!
O'Lord, You help us make such a wonderful life come true.
    Today, as we start out as husband and wife.
Grand is Your stand of love. Honour. And obey.
Grand is our plan to love each other this way.

                     Cont.

Kevin Randall

O'Lord, You are such a wonder, so true:
    Grand are the mountains, You made so high.
    Grand are the stars, You color the sky.
    Grand is Your magestic view.
Grand is Your flame, and You!
With our true hearts, we confess, we thank You for what You bless.
There is no grand love greater than You.
So, today, we pledge our hearts to You, when we say, "I do."
Grand is Your name! Grand is Your flame! Shine on!
Grand, O'Lord, You are such a wonder! Grand is, "I love you!"
"Grand!   Grand!   Grand!"

"Lost Family Prayer"

1) Worked at a faith-based worksite, so we were kept inspired by being routinely challenged to tell an example story of "what?"/ "who?" we witnessed that "couldn't care more" of fulfilling our institution's core values; 2) One example that kept coming back to me is the Biblical passage about the prodigal son; thus, 3) the prayer that each father and son might have shared from different vantage points . . . so, we can all go home again someday, without family taking sides, just doing the right thing through atonement and acceptance and unconditional love.

O' Divine Savior, grant that I may seek
Your haven of strength and courage when I grow weak.

When I have lost touch of Family, or one who has gone astray,
How empty I feel. Thus, I yearn for your loving, caring way.

I pray to be Home with Family again, to feel their endearing embraces.
I rejoice, Oh! Lord, and pray to remain in Your and their ever-caring graces.

Guide us all safely Home to You –
Our loving Father in Heaven – and on Earth, too! Amen.

"With Angel's Care"

1) I imagined a pure picture of "Mother and Babe" delicately bonding with the assurance of joy cradling this new family addition; 2) Working in healthcare settings, many employees see this sight routinely, a nurse or biological mother holding a babe in the hospital nursery rocking chair. One day, I just came upon this awesome sight of a nurse rocking a babe just right, and the way the sunlight hit through the window, it cast "angel wings" across the room. 3) Made me think, are all OB/GYN nurses or neonatal nurses "real mothers" or just "guardian angels?" If not a mother herself, maybe this is what one might be thinking, to have a child of her own to hold?

When you hold a babe in your arms, you cradle her softly.
She calms to your charms that has blest you so heavenly.

Your heart is such a jewel to thine, your motherly loving so divine.
Tender is your caress, serene is your softly tone.
Desires you confess, feelings that this child, like the rest, one to be your own.

You have handled so many newborns that have grown through the ages.
Passing from nursery to youth, to teen; then, onto adult phases.
Viewing one by one, all go on to some other mother's home lot, whereas they belong.
Keeping tabs on them, like their real mother, which you are not . . . woe, the same ol' song.

For now, you're serving the precious needs of these mothers' babies.
And how! You're nurturing these sacred seeds of other ladies.
Face a labor career of sharing so much, love and time on loan.
Embrace daily prayer for Him to hear, "Lord, I pray for one of my own!"

"This, my Lord, would fulfill my life completely."
To have, to hold, if You will – to cherish so sweetly.
Remembered your dream of the past: 'a dolly so real' . . .
Now, that time has encumbered by so fast: "My own baby to feel!"

Please bless me with purpose, clearly understood.
No more fear of loneliness, just pure motherhood!
Fill my life with happiness, a child of love to bear.
All from Angel's care, a child's love, so fair.

You repeat to the Lord, this daily vow you keep.
You stay the vigil onward, a prayer endowed before each sleep:
"Entrust a new life for me . . . to love, to share."
"Bless me, Lord, with my own Angel baby, from Heaven above . . . to love, to care!"

"Yes! No. Maybe?"

1) I always feel God gives us one of three answers when we ask "Why?" or "When" or "Who?" 2) It is up to us to take step back from the situation at hand and look at a wider perspective to have an epiphany and get a wiser view on making choices and wanting the "right" answer; 3) Ps 27:14 "Wait for the Lord. Be strong and take heart." MATT 7:7-8 "Ask, Seek, Knock," and accept His answer of "Thy will be done!"

Did you know that I was on my way? On to see you?
Thought we could talk some today? To share a few.
Traveled through the cold and snow. Didn't care how the wind blew.
Then the traffic got real slow. A train came into view.

Pre-scheming of our time together. All was going great.
Cold-streaming out in this artic weather. Now, I'm running late.
Wondered aloud, "Oh, Creator, what's next? How could this happen to me?"
Couldn't call from this car crowd, nor text. Sure confounded my misery!

Now, I tried to remain so calm. Keep it all sane. And inside.
How could this phone in palm, be my wrath, my bane? I did chide.
Then I said a quick psalm. In God, I did confide.
Staring at the weather, not so balm. Took it all in stride.

Oh, when one is in a fix; when feeling defeat.
Add Smile and Prayer to the mix; helps you compete.
The time was now ten to six. Cryin' eyed, I wrestled in my seat.
Joy and Peace were in my tricks. I realized, now I was getting cold feet.

Noticed that the train did not move. Still sitting at the crossing gate. Stopped and blocked on the tracks dual groove. Seething, a view I was coming to hate.
Suddenly I cried out aloud, "Is this Your Plan? Is this true, no fun with my playmate?"
Ironically, replied from the Heavenly Man, "Thy Will Be Done! <u>You</u> will have to wait."

Other cars, in time, were now turning about. His answer for the mad.
So I took my turn in line, to also get out; His guiding me to be glad.
"No meeting tonight." This train changed my route. Not happy, but not so sad.
"Amen! Alright!" my refrain. I was agreeing with a shout. "So Be It!" It ain't all bad.

Although our time did not come to pass; at least for today.
I relaxed my mind from being crass; His answer: I needed to turn away.
I really did desire to see you, My Lass. Yet, I heeded what He had to say.
That I must use patience, show some class. Listen, to Follow in His Way.

Thus, on this cold, fierce day, I found my destiny.
Prayers and Peace answered, "When?" "What?" "Why me?"
No matter what makes us stand still, it is clear to see.
We must follow His Will: to hear "Yes!" "No." Or, "Maybe?"

"Peace Quest March"

1) Written well over a decade ago, this poem is so relevant in today's American society, that we must overcome hatred, racism, bullying, and bias; 2) Be an advocate for social justice in your honesty march and be a role model in your actual every day friendly actions. 3) Through you, and me, we can make a difference in the world, locally and globally. *Arthur James Balfour ~ "The best thing we can give our enemy is forgiveness; to an opponent, tolerance; to a friend, your heart; to a child, a good example; to yourself, respect; and to all men, charity."*

"Peace Quest March"

When eyes can't meet   our hands don't greet
       And there is no connection.
When hearts won't touch   hate is too much
       And greed is our affliction.
Tempers run short   we rush to court
       And self-egos are the reflection.
We preach for peace   but break our lease
       And push our way around.
We wish to end   try to shake this evil trend
       And move to higher ground.
We drop the mad   ditch being sad
       And ring our peace-bell sound.

Joy! Hopes plan to be found   friendships can abound
And Peace is our Honour Code! And Peace is our Mother Lode!
We must march on in Peace!

We pray for truce from any ruse   to unlight the fuse, stop the abuse
       Our quest is to get along.
Freedom rings now   we talk somehow
       to right our every wrong.
How sweet an ally   to meet eye to eye
       To overcome hate and war's test.
We now shake hands   unite our lands
       And be as one in this peace quest.

Joy! Hopes are found!   Friendships do abound!
And Peace is our Honour Code! And Peace is our Mother Lode!
We must march on in Peace!

"Seasons Of Beauty"

1) By now, you see the subject trend of most of my prose is the love for all four annual seasons, (many more "titled" seasons could have been included; et al, football, positive road improvement construction, fishing, etc!); 2) We usually find at least one negative in a changing variable season, yet the positives outweigh our conflicted joy; 3) So, go enjoy, absorb, and live it up in each season and the beauty it beholds!

"Seasons Of Beauty"

WINTER. SUMMER. SPRING. FALL.
'Tis the Season of Beauty to thank God for it all!
No matter the reason. Whatever the Season for awe!
We bend our knees, and thank Him, for...
    Springs's bees. Summer's breeze. Fall's trees. Winter skis.
Yes! We thank God for them all!
    Thankful, His every Season of B-E-A-U-T-Y, fills mind, soul, heart:
B for Being – the circle of Seasons exist, to end and then re-start;
E for Earth – true nature's miracles consists through God's a la carte;
A for Alpha – All from Genesis, His Beauty comes first;
U for Unique – Each and every imprint, good to worst;
T for Time – to measure all God's magic artwork within;
Y for Young at Heart – to treasure each scenic beauty as a kid again!
God's beauty scenes, some frail or bold, are an awesome sight to behold!
Yes! We thank God for them all!

We journey along Life's annual trail. Each day, more colour comes alive.
It's intended for us that He means to unfold more beauty, as we look or drive.
To see as much as His Seasons of Beauty, as through His eyes.
'Tis the moments and reasons to thank God, truly as our daily exercise.
Cold Winter glittered, snowy nights. Warm Summer sails and iced-teas.
Bold Spring littered in flowery sights. Swarm Autumn Fall trails and piled leaves.
'Tis the Season of Beauty to Thank God for them all!
WINTER. SUMMER. SPRING. FALL.
Yes! We must thank God for them all!

Kevin Randall

"Live-On Legacy"

1) Most of us experience an American eulogy, whether perusing an obit or participating at a "live' celebration of someone's special life; 2) In this case, I personally heard all the charming, envious attributes that made a father be a real "Daddy." What better tribute than to make me desire to do my best in how I live my life, to be a proud role model in such an everlasting, endearing way also. 3) "Old Indian Saying ~ "When you are born, you cried, and the world rejoiced! Live life so that when you die, the world cries, and you rejoice!" *Meng Tzu ~ "A Great Man is he who does not lose his child's heart."*

"Live-On Legacy"

Just came back from a Eulogy.
About a Great Dad. A Live-On Legacy.
He sure was a Great Man!
Someone who did care.
He sure was a Great Man!
      One Life . . . I'd like to compare.

To be a Great Dad.   Such a loving Man.
To be a Great Dad.   If only I can . . .
One with a kind heart, who's fun and fair.
One Life. One Heart. A Great Man.
      For others to yearn to share.

A true Live-On Legacy.
A Great Man!   It can be me . . .
To be that Parent of Love, if only, in memory.
A Living Eulogy.   A Live-On Legacy.
About a Great Man!   If only I can . . .
What a Great Man to be!

Each Star-Light our own effigy of Fate.
How Bright our Star is our own Legacy slate.
It's the Stars amongst the World that makes us especially Great!

Each Star, our own striving prophecy.
We create our own living Eulogy.
Thanks to a Great Man, for his light to help me see.
What a Great Dad! What a Great Man!
What a Live-On Legacy!
He lit the World! . . . And, so I can!
O'Lord, let a Great Live-On Legacy live on with me!

Kevin Randall

"Mind - Heart - Soul"

1) We tend to return to family and home when we get back to basics in trying times. How awesome, if you have family to return to; 2) and, can give you the mental positive support, unconditional love from the heart, and faithful support for the soul to comfort us in time of need; 3) By using all our senses, we can reach self-actualization of peace of mind, compassion of heart, and warmth of soul.

Family. Sisters, Brothers, Dad, and Mother.
Not too far from your <u>mind</u> with each other.
Even if one to stray, then it is one to not be hesitant to find.
Being Family is always on your <u>mind</u>, they be so ever present and so kind.
Life lessons learned from the love they think, do show, and how you two may bind.

I learned so much from you, my Brother.
How not to be cruel, such as being mad, sad, or a bother.
To let someone into your <u>heart</u>, you just let them go.
Hence, the <u>heart</u> will renew that glow,
As the love returns from apart, and spews to grow.

Love from <u>Mind</u>. <u>Heart</u>. <u>Soul</u>. Each a complement to our being whole.
Whether it is just one, two or all three, reach out to leach out of love's big bowl.
Complete love by adding up our kind gentle <u>mind</u>, warm smart <u>heart,</u> and whole caring <u>soul.</u>

Yes, how three words will ever teach us, as we ever grow!
"I Love You" will always reach us, in how they aver to flow.
Keep filled, your <u>Mind</u>, <u>Heart</u>, <u>Soul</u>; it's just the way to endeavor so.
Through these three ways of <u>mind, heart, soul</u>; all are most important, so let family know.

Allow your deep <u>soul</u> love to really show, all the way through.
Don't lose hope from your <u>mind</u>. Nor lose the love of <u>heart</u>, too.
Yes, shine your faith from your <u>soul</u> so true! Then love is fulfilled true enough for me, from you!

"My Prayer Friend"

1) Through the Stephan Ministry stewardship, I learned the art of being a "listening ear" prayer friend; 2) Through the special one-on-one bonding, I learned to respect the client's confidential communication through just that, by being a good listener; 3) And by being more empathic and accepting of people hurting internally; thus, hopefully <u>both</u> of our lives became more enriched. We are all here on earth for a purpose; why not lift up a friend's spirits!

"... listen in silence ..."

You know what to say, more than the shiny frame on the wall.
You let me be heard with a gentle touch, and smile, and more than I can recall.
You brought me care and comfort today. Trust, care, and comfort when I felt so small.
    Lost in the long grass, I did feel so small. Like I didn't matter at all.
    Stubbed my toe on the rocky road; thus, you helped carry my load.
    Through your faith and ministry, attentive kindness, you let me be me.
    For that, I Thank You and your Friends, too.
No words be spoken, you were taught to Listen in Silence; know what to convey, even if in a soft touch.
I was so lost and broken, down and forgotten; yet, you made specific (11) points to help so much:

    1) You were there to help me through it all;
    2) No matter how I vented to you, I recall;
    3) Through pain and fears.
    4) In rage and with plenty of tears,
    5) Through your faith, bended me an ear.
    6) No matter how small or tragically, you kept returning throughout the year.

Just Three Words

Listening in Silence, with your group of Faith Friends,
I felt your prayers of solace, empathy, no matter how each visit ends.

You taught me how to pray that my heart was worth to be saved, from cradle to grave.
Yes! God holds my heart; to be my cure. Yet, you lent an ear and hand to re-assure.

7) I now keep looking for your return smile,
8) To lighten the shadow at my door.
9) You are the ray of light, to get me through each mile that Life has in store.
10) You know what to say, my Silent Friend, now and at the end, as you did before.
11) Listen in Silence, as my true prayer friend, evermore!

As I said, when I stumble on rocky road, you are there to help carry my load.

When I felt dead, when I was lost in weeds so tall, I was feeling so small.
When my faith had fled, you pulled up through your words and deeds, through it all.
You let me rant and rave. You let me be myself. To be so brave.
Taught me that my life is a Soul worthy to save.
When I was broken, so forgotten, lonely in every way,
I was given new hope, good hope for another day.
Again, You came to my door with a smile and more.
Tho', Listening in Silence, you held out your hand, and that bending ear.
I felt so much nearer, for real, not to pretend,
To accept Our God so much clearer, because of your silence and zeal, My Dear Prayer Friend!

"My Daily Devotions"

1) I thought I would humbly, publically, reveal a very rare introspective, personal part of me; 2) By adding the "backbone" of faith ritual I exercise twice a day, morn and eve; 3) Figuring God gave me the same 24 hours each day as everyone else, so I can give him back a few minutes of personal prayer time. (The same holds true with our weekly worship service; He gave us all 168 hours per week to live, I truly am enriched giving Him back 1 hour of thanksgiving prayer and rejoicing in song and His Word with others at the celebration of Mass; 3) Learned and honed my daily prayers from my "Earth Angels" (you know who are), and the positive role modeling you exhibited through the years. DEUT 4:29 ~ ". . . from there you seek God, and you will find Him if you look for Him, with all (mind), heart, and soul."

Just Three Words

"My Daily Devotions"

We all can pray in special thought or word.
Be it your own simple way, to be so daily heard.
To find God in each day, in Heart, in Soul, and in Mind.
Sharing this, what I daily say, it's so awesome what I do find!
Sacred Heart of Jesus, I place my trust in Thee.
"Send forth Your Light, Your Word, Your Truth onto me. Let them guide me." (Ps 43:3)
Thank you for your beautiful, bountiful blessings of yesterday. O'Jesus, please bless me with more today.
I pray to St. Christopher to help carry those in life journey with Safety, Respect, and Pride on their daily ride.
Lord, Bless my family (so named here), with good health, wealth, and joyful happiness to those so dear.
My intercession favors are through St Jose' de Escriba, Patron Saint of ordinary workers, who toil when others ain't.
To be a most faithful, loving servant of the Lord;
To be a most loving, caring father, guide and mentor;

Cont.

To be the best (vocation) at Work,
to my Staff, my Facility,
and the Company I keep in good faith;
to be the best person I can be, to love and be loved. Amen.
Here is where to Thank a special family and friend.
Sweet Holy Mary, I pray that the 7-fold blessings of the Holy Spirit work through me! Wisdom, Understanding
Knowledge, Fortitude, Counsel, Piety, and the Awe of His Presence! Any other blessings by You, be never ending.
Thank you for your kind, caring, compassionate manner, to help me through this day in a same positive, humble way.
Then, here is my special tribute, to my parents (now deceased).
I touch my Mom's worn purse strap,
And my Papa Joe's old ball cap,
to feel the love they brought forth, with increasing joy in each new day's worth.

Now stay with me, these daily Prayers take only a few minutes to complete. To gain His Mighty Spirit through this small feat!
I continue on, and read the daily devotional from "Our Daily Bread." Placing myself in the Story/Prayer and what's said.
Finish with a potent encore with the "7-Second Prayer," to see that

God does move me and to show Him that I truly do care:

"Lord, I love you and I need you. Come into my heart, and bless me, my family, my home, my friends, in Jesus' name. Amen."

Favorite Scripture I then do recite. Great insight! **ASK, SEEK, KNOCK** (Matt 7:7-8) Powerful, my Jesus is such a rock!
"Ask, and it will be given to you; Seek, and you will find; Knock, and the door will be open to you.
For everyone who Asks, receives; he who Seeks, finds; and to him that Knocks, the door will be opened."
Bestowing on St. Jude, to Pray for us, a NOVENA Prayer, (found in a church pew).
Knowing that fate would have me find his prayer of care, for me, for many, or just a few.
Glowing follow-up with an "Our Father," "Hail Mary," and a Glory Be" . . .
Now, you know what starts and fills my day, each day for me! So, how do you pray, too?

PS: A special heart-felt 'Thank You' to all my "Earth Angels" who have helped me form my faith-filled life, in prayer, and through prayer. Absolutely, know that I still love and care! I do pray for you, too!

"Kids Teach Us"

1) Kids can teach us by reflecting back what we teach them, so "listen to them and heed;" 2) Also, remember to say those important evening prayers with them as a daily ritual, just like brushing the teeth before bedtime; 3) and, maintain positive adult role modeling. Children are always watching, listening, and learning by our parental actions and words. Don't lose the daily opportunity to be humble, smile, and learn from our next generational geniuses, too!

The ever day parent scene should be there.
I mean, it is in the "how" and "when" that is shown that you care.
Make it a daily apparent plan, no matter "where."
Teach a child 'how to pray,' by "what" you share.
The night time prayers are best to be said, kneeling by their waiting bed.
It's not all in "what" they say, it's rather more important by your leading actions, instead!

> "Angel of God, my Guardian dear,
> To whom God's love commits me here.
> Ever this night be at my side, and light and guard and rule and guide. Amen!"

"Now I lay me down to sleep.
I pray the Lord, my soul to keep.
Guard me Jesus through the night,
And wake me with the morning light. Amen!"

Then end your tender care kneeling with "something said," of that day each of you are thankful for.
Again, the "prayers for" that they do send, our children near abed, are now ever grateful so much more.
Let them voice the choice of blessed words in their own right.
They will rejoice to learn to pray as 'pj' dressed, again with you, on another night.

Recite prayers, "Our Father," "Hail Mary," "Glory Be."
Each night, added vows to enrich your child's mind, heart, soul by these three.
Might they sleep so much better; with that night time kiss 'n' hug part, and this prayer letter!

Kevin Randall

"The Free Spirits" (Epigram)

1) A "teen years" fictional version of a main Biblical character story, as told in today's present era; 2) Respectfully, there may be a lot of ironies involved in our everyday living; 3) and, the best part to report is, the story never gets old, nor ceases . . . How, awesome "The Free Spirits" saga will carry on to be continued down the road. AMEN!

"... The Good News is too good to keep to ourselves . . . thus, keep the faith, pass it on, keep smiling . . ."

ONCE UPON A TIME, the son in the Goode Family . . . JC went straight down the narrow, winding road. He was swift and direct, and, yet being a good soul, always navigated safely, and bade good cheer to all!

Not having his full license just yet, JC mostly went mudding on the back roads with his multi-toned old pick-up. The truck's driver side door especially had been painted over so much. Thus, the rainbow-shaped lettering was hard to make out 'til you drew closer, and could then distinctly follow the door script: "Salvage All! Father & Son."

Another memorable trait about the pick-up that JC steered was the windshield. JC always looked forward out his big windshield to see the next best great adventures that lie ahead, even though strewn with obstacles and opportunities alike. Oh, he didn't mind glancing o.c. in the wee smaller rearview mirror to see what's been historically traveled, too. His other driving focus was his incessant calling out to see how his pet passenger in the truck bed was faring. Bo, one of his sheep flock, was always nearby, 'cause they were great BBF (Best Buds Forever) since birth. JC had an innate sense that he knew that Bo would be having fun being shepherded around; so much that JC would not hear a beep out of him as they were together. Trusting in JC so devoutly, forever, together, they rambled along the trails.

Now as the story goes, JC's Mother Em, and Papa Joey were well aware that JC drove on and on and on. His loving parents would always encourage him; indeed, by the frequency they requested JC to go to town to deliver letters, miraculously run errands on time, and still be back home for a late supper. Also, they oft urged him to look in on all sorts of folks in that territory.

However, JC's fave errand was to be a "grocery-getter," fetching bread and wine, etc. Also, fishin' was on his parents "to do" list, since a usual special staple was the Friday Fish Fry ritual treat! Other times, JC was found donating time and resources at the local homeless shelters, halfway homes, and health clinics. This young teen was all so busy, trying to role model for all others, always being meaningful and fruitful. Leaving each visit a better place than when he found it.

Mother Em always could sense when JC was nearing home on his return home trips. She would go outside and look out into the distance for his long locks flowing out the pickup window in the wind as he sped up the lane. She'd yell out to Papa Joey, "Here comes the son!" Joey would look up from his carving wood and answer, "So Be It!" Em would just roll her eyes every time he spoke such "Latinese."

Now, when JC would stop his truck long enough to reassure his Mother

Em that he obediently did pass on the scripted messages, JC would usually have a new parable to tell of whom he came across on his much traveled paths. Even included a detailed recount on what was happening in the village square.

Em, by now, knew that JC was such a free spirit, she knew that he'd always stop at the church, too, and hang out with some of the older guys, who thought they were so much smarter than JC. Mother Em would remind him, "I don't want you to learn such worldly ways at your age." JC would diligently respond, "Oh, I can hold my own in their game of 'Jeopardy!' I will always remain true to you and honour you, my Mother and my Father Goode!' Mother Em affirmed his declaration, "Yeah, good!"

After a particular early winter return trip, Mother Em said, "Why don't you go out and find your father out back and help him. He's taken on another part-time job branching out, 'tis the Christmas Yuletide season so near." She went on to add, "He needs help! Seems like he's whittling and fiddling sticks to make some family portraits of us. He also thinks some village people would actually want to acquire a scenic picture of our family made of wood! And, stand-alone novelty statues, too! What is he gonna think of next? He's so nostalgic, stuck in the past. He still pictures you as a young baby, JC!"

"Geez, Mother, doesn't Papa know that I am much older, wiser, and worldy?" JC interjected.

"Yes, son. So do I. You have matured so fast; beyond belief!" I remember just yesterday when you were my early Christmas present, born on that same day! What a holiday spectacle! Why, the whole town reminds me every year of our nativity," she exclaimed. "So it's your birthday reeeallly soon!" They all seem to mark their calendars, like it's just as important as it is to us! How awesome is that?"

"Now, go help your father with those carvings, after you tell me what birthday gift can I get you, my son, who has everything!" Mother Em repeated with a smile. JC stopped and turned around to look her directly in the eye and said to her, "The same as last year, World Peace!" Then he wandered off to see his father to honour his mother's wishes, as she nodded with silent approval.

As JC sneaked up on his Father Joey working in the wood shed, he boldly announced, "I am here!" Father Joey startled from his tasks at hand, looked up and responded, "JC, you always do arrive as a pleasant surprise! Look here, I am working up some carvings of our first family Christmas together! Why, next time you journey off to town, take your Cousin Johnnie with you and market some of these novelties." JC reassured his father, "Surely, I will help you! And with Cuz Johnny's help, we'll be sure to make a splash!" Papa Joey smiled with a proud sparkle in his eye.

Then, since he didn't ever have a lot of face time with JC, Papa Joey went on, "Ever thought what you might do when you grow up? You know that you can't always go muddin', fishing, and hanging out with rock bands like The Saints and The Magi. Heck, who ever heard of a rocker's groupies twelve in number? How's that lead singer, Pete, doing anyway? No denying, he does rock!"

JC liked the fact that his father and mother took a keen interest in his activities, and that they came to know some of his closest buds. "Pete is solid. And as far as those Maji, such wise guys. I only hung out with them once that I recall. They're too far out East," JC said. "Papa Joey, I think people will remember The Saints by their catchy lyrics. They're sticking together alright, name and all. One of the band is being a renegade, though, so I know he will be parting ways with them someday soon."

JC went on to define the band, "The lead four are the main vocals you will hear the most: Matty, Marcos, Lucas, and Jon. Their works are widely known! Their groupies are growing by the droves!" He went on to boast, "The others also have proven themselves to be very important messengers to make the band such a success. Power is in numbers, right Father?!" Papa Joey echoed, "So Be It!" JC just rolled his eyes and went on with the tasks at hand.

Father and son, working together in concert, completed their tasks miraculously swiftly. So much so, that while Papa Joey busied himself with more of his carvings, he would occasionally glance over and catch JC drawing in the sand. "Look Father, I created a star with our family monogram on it: 'Em-Pa-Thee.' "

"You should mold these wooden stars with such an emblem. Why, they would be a big hit at market!" Father answered, "Why, son, I think you are onto something. We could have folks place them on their trees, along with these family etchings. I like your thinking."

JC went onto ask, "For my Birthday this year, can I be the one who places the star on our family's Christmas tree?" Papa Joey responded, "You better go ask your mother. And whatever answer she replies, my blessing, too. "So Be It!" JC just rolled his eyes as he ran to the homestead. Ran so fast he lost one of his flip-flops. Father Joey just smiled, knowing that he and Mother Em helped raise such a free spirit.

JC dashed past the gate, through the front door, leaving it ajar. He yelled out to Mother Em, "Father has sent me!" Dashing in so hurriedly, he surprised Mother Em, who was hanging out with Auntie Lizzie. Actually, both were in awe of such a grand entrance that they spilt their wine glasses. "Say 'Hey!' to your Auntie Lizzie, as she mopped up some. Now, she's older so you will have to speak up some. She had her son, your Cuz Johnnie, truck her over for a spell, while he wants to go hang out with you. Now, what's this fuss about your father?"

Before JC could answer, Auntie Lizzie saw JC and interjected, "Johnnie brought me over in his old beater pick-up to spend time with your Mother Em. It is such a Happy Hour!"

"Hello, Auntie Lizzie! Good to see you. Glad that I can hang out with Johnnie, too. We'll probably go to the beach," JC said.

Mother Em yelled out to JC, "Born in the Barn? Shut that door." JC retorted, "Yes, Mother. Your wish is my command." Kidding her further, he went on, "You know, when one door closes, another opens." Mother Em answered, "I guess I deserved that. Ask, a smarty question, and I will receive one back. Well, close that door please, you ne'er know who might come a knockin'!"

Mother Em noticed that the cupboard was bare, no more wine bottles on the top shelf. So she directed JC, "Be a good son and go get more vino! You might as well get some bread too. Fish Friday coming up soon as well. We might as well prepare for a feast. You can't always guess how many hungry souls come round here." JC retorted, "I will team up with Cuz Johnnie and head toward the village to gather a feast for our 'unexpected' crowd!"

Mother Em added, "I know that your cousin really is quite a noted outdoorsman type, so have him catch some of those big fishies with ya!" Then, why don't you two stop over and see friends your own age, like Marty and Merry? Heaven knows what you hear and say when you meet those older guys down by the church. Why, Auntie Lizzie and I remember that you left quite a ruble scene down by the church one time. A downright embarrassing riot ensued! Now off with you. Please stop over and see Marty and Merry, 'cause I did hear that their brother was gravely ill. They will need some cheering up."

JC noticed in the distance that Cuz Johnnie was truckin' back nearer to the home from the wilderness growth. JC gave his mother his agreement to fulfill her wish lists and headed for the door. Closing the door tightly behind him, he and Bo ran to his pickup truck. JC gave Bo his friendly look as they headed on to meet up with Cuz Johnnie, on the trail.

As he approached Cuz Johnnie's rusted ol' pickup, Johnnie performed some donuts in the sand. Then JC waved Cuz Johnnie over to follow him in making a new trail where no one had ever ventured. JC slowed his speed some, since Johnnie's jalopy was held together only by rust, bondo, and duct tape, and not so worthy to keep up the same speed. Heck, that pickup had many holes and cracks even in the windshield. So much so that the wind made Johnnie's hair frizz up, plus remain matted together, after each trek. So much so that JC and fellow teens always teased Johnnie about wearing bugs for hair gel!

That was such a popularly noted trademark for Johnnie that JC urged Cuz Johnnie to try out for The Saints band. Wild-haired Johnnie would always repeat the same claim, "I'm not worthy. I follow my own beat of the drum, enough that I got my own gig playing at the local Desert Inn.

Booked for forty days!" JC, taking after his father, nodded, "So Be It!" Johnnie, knowing that that retort was coming, just rolled his eyes and they kept on truckin'.

Meanwhile, back on the trail, Johnnie yelled out, "Where we headin'?" JC shouted back, "To the shore. To town. To explore. To friends. Just leading on in a new way. Now, follow me!"

Arriving at the shoreline together, JC climbed out of his pickup. Cuz Johnnie jumped out of his and ran toward the beach, yelling, "Let's take a dip!" Even though it was freezing out, JC agreed to take the polar plunge, too. Cuz Johnnie skidded on thin ice, found the gap to plunge in feet first, and came up with a fish in tow. What a blessing! JC re-enacted this same feat, echoed, "Yeah, It's another miracle!" However, Mother Em said we have a lot more mouths to feed, so keep on dipping." This time it was Cuz Johnnie's turn to profess, "So Be It!" JC just rolled his eyes and smiled as they both kept fishing. More on these two free spirits' story to come.

Back at the ranch, Papa Joey took a labor break and headed in to check in on Mother Em. While he passed a clearing on the other side of the stable, he caught sight of smoke arising near the top of Mt. Mosely. This reminded Joey of his pre-marriage days when he went camping and hiking alone throughout the land. He reminded himself aloud, "Quite a traveler in my day!" Then he remembered that when he had dated Em, he would hitch up only one horse so that she could ride while he ambled alongside. Just then, another big wisp of smoke aroma rustled him out of his 'past-days' dreams. He squinted once again toward Mt. Mosley, and this time saw real fire and brimstone ablaze in dem' der' hills.

Joey ran in to alert Em. Ran so fast that he forgot (again) to shake off all the saw dust from his clothes before he had reached the backdoor. Entering, hailed out, "Mother! Mother Em!" I swear I just saw Mt. Mosely on fire!" His acclamation was so loud that even Auntie Lizzie heard him, so she affirmed, "Oh, that's Ol' Man Mosely! I call him Moose. He's such a bull-headed figure."

She went on, "He's always taking some campers up in the hills and pitching tents, regardless of the weather! Reckon' that his campfire caught some brush afire." Mother Em chided in, "Mosley just ain't normal. Why rumour has it, that he actually carves on rocks. You, a husband of wood; him, a profiteer, making something out of stone!" Papa Joey, humbled, mumbled, "What the . . .?"

Auntie Lizzie chimed in, "Moose never had much schooling. Some people think him a fool!"

Mother Em, continued, "Yeah, some say he can't count to ten. That's as far as he got on them stone carvings! Did some other scribblings, too."

"We'll all find out soon enough what all his fuss is about when he comes off his mountain top!" Auntie Lizzie added.

Papa Joey mumbled, "So Be It!"

Mother Em, and even Auntie Lizzie, nodded as they rolled their eyes. Auntie added, "Moose is quite an idol to some with his 'blaze and glory.' "

Em retorted, "A real leader, I'd say." She went on, "Thy shall know more about Mosely soon enough when we get to talk to the rest of his camping party, when they come off that mountain pulpit." Papa Joey agreed, "So

Be It!" Mother Em just rolled her eyes at that typical Joey "Latinese." She double-rolled her eyes, aghast at seeing all that sawdust strewn like ashes, all about the home. "Go clean up!"

"Papa, you know we got to also get ready for JC's birthday! Our anniversary, too, mind ya'! Hint! Hint! Yet, JC, our son, comes first. He's such an angel!" Papa heading for the washroom, stated, "JC wants to proudly hang up one of our family carvings on a tree for his main present." Em nodded in agreement, and said, "What else can you get a son who seems like he has everything?" She went on and yelled out since Papa was cleaning up, "I know, why don't you surprise him and make up added carvings of animals, like Bo and others, to make a real outdoor nature scene?"

Auntie Lizzie, hearing the last part, butted in again, "I know a guy, who knows of a guy, who knows this ol' man, nicknamed Zoo-ah, who has two animals of every type known to man." Em laughed, "A real zoo is right! I know JC would like a carving of his pet sheep, Bo, and other wild game!" Auntie Lizzie rambled on, "Yeah, Zoo-ah has been known to parade them around. Why, legend has it he has taken them on tours, land and by sea!" Papa Joey, re-entered the sitting room, interjected, "That would be a surprise nice treat for JC. I hope I can get Bo to pose in one spot long enough for a carving. He is such a free spirit, too, just like JC!"

Mother Em added, "Why, we could hang the star on the top of that big fir out in the front yard! And string some other carvings around and around toward the base. This way, we could gaze out our window to enjoy, while all world travelers could take in this new Christmas scene tradition as they pass by. What joy to all!"

Papa whispered, "So Be It!" Mother Em just rolled her eyes as she encouraged Lizzie to start the networking in motion to have all presents completed and collected in grand anticipation of JC's birthday celebration.

***

As time went on, many stories and tales of the Goode family proclaimed just how much of the free spirits they really were. This here legendary story will be continued if, "Natures willing and the creek don't rise." Especially where Cuz Johnnie and JC were last depicted as the free spirits out in the wilderness, blazin' new trails for others to follow. And, if God willing, Papa Joey was to catch up with the flock of wild to carve more creatures. The trending legacy was that Papa Joey usually got the last word in on whatever Mother Em uttered, with his fulfilling conclusion, "So Be It!"

Now, it's your turn to just roll your eyes and learn more about what's next for these Goodes ... "The Free Spirits!" Stay tuned for more Goode news.

About the Author

Kevin Randall hails from Midwest farming country. Born and raised in an era when hard work ethic was commonplace in all sorts of cultures, he performed community work and delivered customer service excellence. Randall grew up in America's rock 'n' roll generation, when a song's lyrics could be heard and understood, and when the best movie stars were idolized in black and white cinema.

The literary bug bit during those simple years and ingrained itself into many of Randall's earlier writings and continues to this day. As a romantic hopeful, he firmly believes we all have a story to tell. Herewith are parts of that story intertwined with the blessings of talents and words shared by many personal and public contacts along the way.

Although his loving parents are deceased, Randall credits much of his formative years to their faith-filled upbringing, along with the help of his siblings, who loved the cultural arts. Yet to reach full maturity, sustainability, and self-actualization, he still yearns and fights for the day when he can claim and role-model these same winning qualities. With continued prayers, support, and love from family, extended family, and charismatic friends, he knows that Heaven is the goal to strive for here on Earth!

Kevin Randall

www.ingramcontent.com/pod-product-compliance
Lightning Source LLC
Chambersburg PA
CBHW071622080526
44588CB00010B/1232